*Critical Guides to French Texts*

*Critical Guides to French Texts*

EDITED BY ROGER LITTLE, WOLFGANG VAN EMDEN, DAVID WILLIAMS

OYONO

# Une vie de boy
*and*
# Le Vieux Nègre et la médaille

**Patrick Corcoran**

School of English and Modern Languages
University of Surrey Roehampton

Grant & Cutler Ltd
2003

© Grant & Cutler Ltd 2003

ISBN 0 7293 0437 X

DEPÓSITO LEGAL: V. 334 – 2003

Printed in Spain by
Artes Gráficas Soler, S.L., Valencia
for
GRANT & CUTLER LTD
55-57 GREAT MARLBOROUGH STREET, LONDON W1F 7AY

For Camille

# Contents

## Prefatory Note

References to *Une vie de boy* are to the Presses Pocket edition (re-published 1970) and references to *Le Vieux Nègre et la médaille* are to the 10/18 edition (re-published 1986). References of the type (7, p.99) relate to works listed in the Select Bibliography.

The text of this study makes constant references to Blacks, Whites, Africans, French etc. I am aware of the risks involved in adopting such blanket terminology which may not only be seen as blurring important distinctions but also as being, on occasion, inaccurate, inappropriate or even offensive. I have nevertheless decided to follow the example of Oyono himself in this regard and rely on my readers to make the appropriate adjustments and distinctions when they come across such terms.

This study has benefited a great deal from contributions to seminars and class discussions by students and staff of the Modern Languages Department at the University of Surrey Roehampton. I would like to express my thanks and appreciation to them. My sincere thanks are also extended to Professor Roger Little of Trinity College, Dublin whose encouragement and advice have made the writing of it an easier task.

# Introduction

In the space of four years, Ferdinand Oyono, born in 1929, published three novels: *Une vie de boy* (1956), *Le Vieux Nègre et la médaille* (1956) and *Chemin d'Europe* (1960) all of which continue to enjoy a wide readership today. Since 1960, however, Oyono has published nothing further and instead has devoted his energies to a career in international diplomacy and, in more recent years, to the political life of his native Cameroon where he is currently Minister of Culture. 1960, therefore, was something of a watershed in Oyono's personal life as indeed it was for Africa as a whole. It can be seen as marking the point at which he abandoned the strategy of writing fictions about colonial oppression in order to align himself with the political class which was assuming power in post-colonial Cameroon. Needless to say, this study has no comment to make about Oyono the diplomat or Oyono the politician and focuses on the work of Oyono the novelist.

Although Oyono's brief literary career occupied considerably less than a decade it belongs to an extremely important and exciting period in the history of modern Africa. The 1950s were a decade in which the gathering political momentum towards independence for France's African colonies came to be seen as unstoppable. There were one or two notable exceptions, of course, including the Algerian war (1954–1962) which served as much as a reminder of how badly things could go wrong in matters of colonial disengagement as it was, for some, a symbol of rearguard imperialist ambitions. By and large, however, by the 1950s the colonial powers had accepted that they were living on borrowed time. This period of rapid change was also a period in which increasing numbers of African writers began to publish work which, directly or indirectly, mirrored the preoccupations of those striving towards political independence. This is certainly true of Oyono's novels, although it would be more accurate to insist on the social critique in evidence in his writings rather than on any specifically political campaign. Nevertheless, it is among this generation of writers, which includes Sembène Ousmane (Senegal) and Mongo Beti (Cameroon) that Oyono should be firmly located.

This is not to say that African literature in French has no history prior to what Jacques Chevrier has called 'les romans de la contestation' (*8*, p.99). Previous decades had seen the publication of a considerable body of poetry and a number of novels, some of them, like René Maran's *Batouala* (1921), quite strongly critical of the colonial régime. If Oyono's own father was to lose his job in the French colonial administration as a result of his son's forays into literature (*21*, p.4), Maran had suffered a similar fate more than thirty years earlier. But Maran is something of an exception and what is far more typical of much of this earlier work is the emphasis writers placed on defining and identifying specifically African cultural values and perspectives on the world. In the face of the dehumanising exactions of the French colonial régime, African intellectuals responded with a philosophically inspired crusade seeking to foreground the contributions which African culture continued to make to universal culture. This was the essential, not to say essentialist, message of the *négritude* movement, which loosely grouped together the largely Parisian-based artists and writers contributing to the review, *L'Etudiant noir* from the mid-1930s onwards.[1] The theme of revolt is certainly present in their work but it tends to take a metaphysical rather than a directly political form of expression. With the passage of time, however, a hardening of political attitudes did occur, although perhaps more spontaneously among Caribbean writers than Africans. It is discernible, for example in a simple comparison of two works by the Martinican poet, Aimé Césaire. Before the war, he had given vent to his anger in poetic form with his *Cahier d'un retour au pays natal* (1939), whereas after

---

[1] Léopold-Sédar Senghor, Léon Damas and Aimé Césaire are generally considered as the founders of the *négritude* movement. Lilyan Kesteloot's *Les Ecrivains noirs de langue française: naissance d'une littérature* (Brussels: Université Libre, 1960) continues to be the work of reference on this subject.

the war, and in the wake of such publications as Frantz Fanon's *Peau noire, masques blancs* (1952), he chose a far more direct form of address in the vitriolic pamphlet *Discours sur le colonialisme* (1955).

But even as late as the 1950s the literary reaction to the injustices of colonial rule continued to be far from heavily politicised. The *négritude* response based on an insistence on the warmth of the African personality and the specificity of African culture, particularly the sense of rhythm and the stress on communal solidarity, had reinforced a tendency to look backwards to a pre-colonial past as a source of inspiration. Nothing could be more natural as a way of refusing the straitjacket of colonialist views and decontextualised representations of the African, than this representation of an African past celebrated by Africans themselves. Hence, from the oral tradition, cycles of folk tales on the one hand, and epics of genealogical and cosmogonical significance on the other, had been transcribed and transposed into literary form by Africans such as Birago Diop since the 1940s onwards. But the tendency to look in the opposite direction, or even to occult an unsavoury political present by focusing on an idyllic vision of Africa, also surfaces in novels which are contemporaneous with Oyono's work. *L'Enfant noir* (1953) by Camara Laye is a case in point. The Guinean author was taken to task by the more overtly political writer, Mongo Beti, for his failure to include in his novel any reference to the political realities of the period.[2] The point here is not to take sides in this debate but to emphasise the fact that two distinct strategies began to surface quite clearly by the mid-1950s. Thereafter, the overtly political response is probably best represented by the novels of Sembène Ousmane, particularly *Les Bouts de bois de Dieu* (1960), while more nuanced novels, such as Cheikh Hamidou Kane's *L'Aventure ambiguë* (1961), which presented the problems in cultural or even spiritual rather than political terms, continued to have considerable influence.

---

[2] Mongo Beti's article on *L'Enfant noir* appears under the initials A.B. (Alexandre Biyidi) in *Trois écrivains noirs* (Paris: Présence Africaine, 1954).

But it would be mistaken to see the legacy of *négritude* as in some way involving a stifling of political responses to colonialism. In many respects, the emphasis on cultural values was of central importance and it should not be forgotten that the crisis which colonialism provoked throughout Africa was also a crisis of culture. Indeed, it is arguable whether the real drama for Africans was not so much the fact of political and economic oppression, which colonialism undoubtedly institutionalised, as the fact that the installation of colonial rule had been accompanied by a systematic refusal to acknowledge that indigenous cultural practices had any value. By refusing to acknowledge the value of African culture and African forms of social organisation the colonialists were, by implication, calling into question the very humanity of the colonised. The distinction I am making here between, on the one hand, the political and economic exploitation suffered by the colonised and, on the other, the disastrous cultural impact of colonisation, is directly reflected in the way the colonisers themselves viewed their enterprise. The wielding of political and/or military power and the material advantages to be gained from a career spent in the colonies were generally presented as merely one side of the coin. The obverse was the *mission civilisatrice*, the 'white man's burden' of bringing civilisation to far-flung corners of the earth. To what extent the latter was a motive for colonial expansion and to what extent it was a retrospective justification for the invasion and conquest of overseas territories is not of direct concern to the present study. But what is important to recognise is the constant interplay, within the colonial context, of the nakedly materialist interests of the colonisers and the potential they had for invoking a higher and purely disinterested purpose as a justification for their actions. It was exactly this fertile terrain of contradictory motivations that Oyono exploited to the full in *Une vie de boy* and *Le Vieux Nègre et la médaille*.

This brief description of the historical and political context within which Oyono was writing his novels is also extremely relevant in other ways. The writing of novels is not an innocent activity taking place in some timeless, asocial vacuum and dealing with eternal and universal values. On the contrary, it is an activity rooted in a social setting which is itself subject to the shaping influence of political forces. This 'social setting' in turn influences the conditions in which texts are produced (who has the educational background, the leisure, the material conditions that make 'writing' possible?); it determines whether or not and in what conditions texts are published (does censorship or self-censorship operate? are publishing houses independent or based overseas?); and it finds itself reflected, refracted or suppressed in the content of the novel. The same notion of 'social setting', similar to or completely different from the 'social setting' of the text's production, will operate upon the reader who comes to read the novel. This time, the 'social setting' will be a determining factor in the novel's availability, either in physical terms (is it in print? does its price render it effectively unobtainable, or unobtainable for certain groups of readers?), or in terms of its status (is it a mainstream canonical text or is it considered marginal and relevant to a minority interest?). Perhaps more significantly, it will determine whether or not, or with what degree of difficulty, the text is 'readable', either in a literal sense (is the population literate? does it read the language of the text?) or on a more figurative level: whether the text can speak across cultural boundaries and whether the internal interplay of voices it orchestrates can awaken any corresponding dialogue between reader and text even though these two may be located in vastly different social and cultural settings.

Where writers and readers are operating within a common cultural tradition and there is a high degree of correspondence between their respective 'social settings', many of the questions raised above seem to have little relevance. They are seen as unproblematic because any cultural tradition has an innate tendency to present its own particularities as natural, if not universal practices. But when the 'social setting' in which texts are produced are so disconnected from the 'social setting' in which they are 'consumed', such questions assume tremendous importance. In the case of Oyono, it is not without significance, for example, that *Une vie de boy* and *Le Vieux Nègre et la médaille* were both written in French, were both written in France and were published by a French publishing house.

As the rest of this study will show, they also work very successfully as novels,[3] but we must also recognise that the novel is a form of cultural expression which has no organic roots in Cameroonian traditions. Oyono's adoption of the colonisers' language and his selection of a relatively high-status genre from the colonisers' own literary traditions, the novel, in order to focus attention on the evils of colonialism, are choices that seem to involve him in subversion on a variety of different levels. It would be a pity if we failed to see this subversion for what it is, simply because the language and the form of expression is so familiar to us, the largely Western consumers who would appear to be its chief audience.

Many of these general considerations point in the same direction and suggest a particular view of literature's purposes and functions, at least for this generation of African texts in French. Firstly, they appear to indicate that questions relating to aesthetics and form are likely to be seen as of lesser significance than questions relating to the representation of socio-political and cultural realities. Secondly, the author's own relation to the texts he has produced and the contexts about which he has written, as well as the reader's or the critic's location in respect of all of this, become themselves important subjects for consideration. It is as though the act of writing these novels and the act of reading them are suddenly imbued with a range of meanings requiring renegotiation; as though they existentially involve authors and readers alike in processes of axiological re-evaluation and cultural repositioning. And finally they invite a reflection on whole range of questions concerning identity and difference. The African novel seems to focus on matters relating to cultural identity and the representation of the Other in particularly acute ways. In this respect, can Oyono's use of the novel really be considered as equivalent to that of any French contemporary we might choose to name: Sartre, Vailland, Queneau or Claude Simon, for example? Or, perhaps more problematically, the Algerian-born Camus or the Irish-born Beckett, who both wrote in French? The range of affiliations and disjunctions, of identifications and

---

[3] Throughout this study, the term 'novel', rather than 'novella', 'narrative' or other alternatives, is applied to both of the texts under consideration.

disaffections which work so as to bind together or to disconnect author and readership, which determine the particular ways language will be invested, passively accepted or actively transformed, and which promote or reject positionings with regard to cultural and political values... all of these inevitably contribute to defining the location inhabited by a given author and they would appear to have particular acuity for the author who has been on the receiving end of colonial rule. Some of the precise ways in which Oyono's novels are embroiled in the complex web of relationships outlined here will, I hope, emerge from the present study.

## 1. Colonial relations

Most non-African readers (and a good many African ones) who turn to Oyono's first novel, *Une vie de boy*, will have little precise knowledge of Cameroon, its history or its peoples. They may even expect that a novel written by a Cameroonian and set in a small West African town during the period of colonial rule might provide them with insights into the daily life of those who had experienced the colonial system at first hand. In many ways, and allowing for fictional transposition and manipulation, this is exactly what the novel does provide. It offers an unflattering and rather harsh portrayal of a number of African characters and their living conditions. But, more interestingly, the novel provides a much richer, more detailed and far more scathing portrait of the European masters. Hence, the majority of readers who engage with the novel may have the uncomfortable impression that the voyeuristic impulse to use fiction as a way of looking into a new and different world is being turned against them. As they follow Toundi's relentless observation of the White colonialists, they may come to feel that it is they themselves who are being subjected to scrutiny. Irrespective of their own ethnic origins or political affiliations, the very fact of belonging to a society that has materially benefited from colonial exploitation may lead many readers to feel something of the power of the gaze that Toundi turns upon his White masters.

But although colonial relationships are at the very heart of *Une vie de boy* and *Le Vieux Nègre et la médaille*, they are never presented in a partisan way or in purely negative terms. On the contrary, Oyono is at pains to demonstrate the fascination that the presence of Europeans (or the prospect of gaining access to Europe in the case of his later novel, *Chemin d'Europe*) could exercise on the impressionable minds of the indigenous population. This is not simply a function of political power. The apparatus of the colonial state, as it is presented in Oyono's work, does not appear to be heavily reliant on military force or technological superiority. Much more significant than such concrete manifestations of power is the *ideological* enlistment of the population into the colonial project by the use of religion and the appeal that is made to the Blacks' desire to be associated with the status and prestige that closeness to the masters brings. It is true that the fear of violence, real or threatened, lurks closely behind this desire for proximity to the Whites, but the temptation to collaborate with colonialism is far more commonly in evidence throughout Oyono's work than any references to organised resistance.

In order to understand the reasons why this might be the case, a few words about French colonial policy may be helpful. One of the frequent justifications for colonial activity produced by the European powers was the notion that it was a duty incumbent upon them to undertake a civilising mission in their colonies. The French version of this *mission civilisatrice* involved a particular emphasis on the assimilation of the colonial subject. The theory was that indigenous peoples should aspire to become sufficiently accultured to French ways and to French language and culture to enable them eventually to be absorbed into French citizenship. Thus, the whole impetus behind French colonial rule was provided by the colonisers' unquestioned belief in the superiority of French culture over the culture(s) of the colonised peoples and the unquestioned assumption that those under colonial rule should strive to become increasingly like their French masters. However wrong-headed such views may appear with hindsight, they were at least based on solid republican principles and the acceptance that colonised peoples would one day be able to enjoy the same liberty, equality and fraternity that the metropolitan French citizen enjoyed. Translated into the world of everyday realities, however, these assimilationist theories could easily become merely an alibi and a way of deferring real progress. It could easily be argued that it was precisely because the road to becoming fully assimilated was so long and arduous and because the colonial subject was not yet ready to exercise the rights and enjoy the advantages that equal status would eventually bring that differential treatment, including all the various forms of political and social discrimination, forced labour, minimal legal rights and so on, could be justified. Assimilation thus remained little more than a promise, but it remained at the heart of the unspoken colonial 'contract'.

This notion of a colonial 'contract' is particularly useful in the attempt to understand the reasons why the two protagonists, Toundi and Meka, seem so willing to collude with their colonial masters. The assumption that a contract exists allows the colonial enterprise to proceed on the basis of collaboration rather than conflict and it helps mask the reality of political and economic inequality behind a façade of socio-cultural difference. What interests Oyono is not denouncing political injustice *per se* but demonstrating the moral and ethical bankruptcy of the whole colonial enterprise.

It is for this reason that both *Une vie de boy* and *Le Vieux Nègre et la médaille* must be considered as essentially social rather than political critiques. They examine in great detail the behaviour of individuals and the social situations in which they operate. They may in the long run invite the reader to interpret this behaviour as significant on a political or ideological level but this is not their ostensible aim. So even if the characters themselves (Toundi, Meka, Kelara) come to a deeper understanding of their situation and recognise the reality of colonial relationships, there are limits to the knowledge they have gleaned and they appear ill-equipped to do anything with it. It certainly stops short of providing a motivation or a means for them to pursue any particular line of action. For Toundi, of course, whatever realisation there is comes too late. But in the case of Meka the sense of disillusionment is far stronger and yet his experiences remain for him essentially sterile. 'A présent je m'en moque [...] Je ne suis plus qu'un vieil homme' (*2*, p.187), he concludes at the close of the novel and in a tone that suggests he has no alternative but to accept not only his own powerlessness in the face of colonial domination but his own inability to explain why the Whites behave as they do. Toundi too, on his deathbed, voices the same fundamental incomprehension: 'Que sommes-nous? Que sont tous ces nègres qu'on dit français?' (*1*, p.13).

What is true for the characters is not necessarily true for readers, however. The mixture of understanding and incomprehension that typify the reactions of Toundi and Meka is a rhetorical strategy consciously adopted by Oyono to underline the true nature of the colonial relationship. Similarly, although their experiences do not lead the characters to a political response, or even to active resistance, this is not to say that Oyono's social critique of colonial relations does not raise political awareness among its readers. Central to Oyono's purpose in both novels is, of course, the presentation of the sorts of relationships that link the coloniser and the colonised and these deserve to be considered now in some detail.

## Une vie de boy

Both as narrator and as participant in the action of the novel, Toundi's role throughout *Une vie de boy* is essentially ambivalent. On the one hand, he is a representative of the African community from which he issues and with which he maintains ties based on family links as well as social solidarity. Many of his reactions and responses to events, and in particular his moments of incomprehension at the way his masters behave, reflect the African side to his nature.[4] But he is also quite clearly differentiated from his fellow Africans. He 'enjoys' a privileged position, firstly as *boy* to Père Gilbert and later to the Commandant, which allows him access to an altogether different world from that which he would otherwise have inhabited. When he eventually voices personal aspirations they are clearly modelled on the life style and the life expectations of his White masters rather than on those of his family and friends. Toundi's is the classic dilemma of a being who is torn between the pull of where he has come from and the fascination of where he would like to go. This radical ambivalence can be traced back to the

---

[4] To speak of an African side to Toundi's nature is, of course, to adopt the essentialist terminology that encourages stereotyping and contributes to the indiscriminate objectification of the Other that Oyono's work attempts to expose. I would nevertheless defend my use of the term here on the grounds that Oyono himself appears to be playing with such categories in his own analysis.

moment early on in the novel when he first exercises a choice. His decision to follow the priest is composed of two distinct elements. It involves a rejection of paternal authority and of his African heritage — he chooses to run away from home on the eve of his initiation — and an espousal of the world of the Whites as well as a desire to experience the way they live: 'J'étais heureux […] j'allais connaître la ville et vivre comme eux' (*1*, p.22). Indeed the substitution of the authority of Père Gilbert for the paternal authority of his natural father indicates quite clearly that Toundi is a willing colonial subject, freely volunteering to accept colonial rule. A good deal of the implicit and explicit criticism that will flow from his experiences gains added strength from the fact that Toundi has willingly colluded with the forces that eventually destroy him. And this allows Oyono to demonstrate that even from within its own assimilationist logic, colonialism must be exposed as a sham.

Toundi's decision to follow Père Gilbert and offer his services to the priest can clearly be seen in symbolic terms. It is as though Oyono were saying, 'let us imagine what would happen to the African who takes the Whites at face value and freely accepts the colonial 'contract''. Moreover, the African colonial subject, so often stereotyped in the colonial imagination as unsophisticated, naive, primitive and childlike, finds a direct correlate in the character of the young, unformed Toundi, who offers himself up to be shaped by the experiences he willingly seeks through sustained contact with the Whites. Thus Toundi and his situation would appear to combine all the required ingredients that will allow Oyono to describe the experiment and complete his demonstration. And the sum of Toundi's personal experiences, his life and the death he suffers as a consequence, can all be read on the same symbolic level as that identified for his original decision. His personal experience can be seen as representative of the global African experience of colonial-ism and the fundamental breach of promise upon which it was predicated.

The fact that colonialist rule involved a contract that would not, could not and perhaps should not, be honoured, is illustrated in every aspect of the colonial enterprise, not least in the ways missionary activity and religion are seen to collude with the secular, military and commercial interests at work. It is little surprise therefore, that religion should play such a key role in the early stages of Toundi's decision to embrace the White man's world. Toundi's first contact with the Whites is through the proselytising efforts of Père Gilbert and, when his offer to serve the priest is accepted, his first home is at the Catholic mission at Dangan where he has the opportunity to observe at close quarters the somewhat unholy behaviour of Père Vandermayer. But although the link between the religious mission and the civil administration is further underscored in the scene describing the Commandant's visit to mass at Dangan, the religious element gradually fades to be replaced by a more overt civil and finally judicial/penal presence. Toundi may be enlisted through the efforts of missionaries but thereafter the weight of colonial power that eventually bears down upon him represents the secular machinery of the civil state.

What is striking about Oyono's presentation of the religious element in colonial life is precisely how unreligious it is. The religious mission is totally devoid of any spiritual content. Indeed, quite the contrary would appear to be true: material and materialistic concerns predominate wherever religion is mentioned. This is reflected in Père Gilbert's tactic for attracting converts during his sallies into the bush: he appears to make no appeal to Christian doctrine and instead he targets children, whom he entices with sugar cubes. Ironically, the distribution of such sweets provokes street-fights among the infants and this in turn sets the adults at each other's throats, an outcome that would seem to be in direct contradiction to the fundamental philosophy behind the teachings of Christianity. Similarly, the two chief characteristics of Père Vandermayer, which Toundi highlights in his journal, are his obsession with money (he insists on collecting the offerings of the congregation at Sunday mass personally: *1*, p.25) and his sadistic penchant for beating his (black) parishioners into finer Christian sentiments (*1*, pp.25–26). But both the likeable Père Gilbert and the fearsome Père Vandermayer are equally responsible for imposing on the community at the mission a régime of relentless hard work for little or no pay. Thus the colonial exploitation of indigenous labour which is so familiar in other contexts appears to be equally true of the religious sphere.

The Commandant's attendance at mass at the mission is undoubtedly the most telling example in the novel of the uses which the colonisers themselves make of religion. For the Whites, mass is essentially an event in the social calendar, although the description of the scene is peppered with reminders of the hierarchical nature of colonial society and the power relations which underpin those hierarchies. For example, the Commandant requires the presence of Toundi, Gosier d'Oiseau demands the presence of his subordinate and even the agricultural engineer insists on being attended by Ondoua, the tom-tom player, presumably as a demonstration of their status as masters. Interestingly enough, throughout this scene, the characters and the actions of the Whites are individualised whereas the Blacks are considered *en masse* as 'une foule grouillante' (*1*, p.51) are referred to as a group or generically as 'les fidèles indigènes [...] Hommes et femmes' (*1*, p.54) and seen as acting in concert. They distinguish themselves from the group only insofar as they have a demonstrable connection with the Whites, and this connection seems to be the source of their identity. Toundi's status as 'boy du commandant' (*1*, p.55) is a case in point.

As a place of social intercourse for the Whites, mass at Dangan is merely an alternative venue to that provided by the *Cercle européen*. It is a place to see and be seen. The Whites parade in uniform or fashionable clothes in order to make a statement about their rank, to impress their neighbours or to facilitate attempts at flirtation. Mme Salvain has designs on the Commandant while Gosier d'Oiseau and the agricultural engineer focus their attentions on the Dubois girls. All of them provide an interesting spectacle for the wife of the Doctor and none seems to show the slightest interest in the religious nature of the event. Indeed, when the mass gets under way it is described in terms of a ballet in which the Blacks alone actively participate as performers while the Whites take advantage of the ceremony to carry on their flirtatious behaviour: 'Là-bas, Gosier d'Oiseau profitait de l'élévation pour presser la main de sa voisine, tandis que les jambes de Mme Salvain se rapprochaient imperceptiblement de celles du commandant' (*1*, p.54).

There is a more sinister side to the scene than this comedy of social manners might suggest, however. For instance, Toundi describes the spatial segregation that operates in the church, with the Whites comfortably seated close to the altar in the transept while the Blacks occupy the nave and have to make do with roughly hewn tree trunks as seats. The Whites also have their own entrance and exit so as to ensure that physical contact with the Blacks is kept to a minimum, yet another blatant contradiction of the Christian message they are supposed to have come together to celebrate. These various forms of segregation are closely policed by the *catéchistes* who act as the henchmen of the priests, supervising events and more than ready to inflict physical violence on any Black who steps out of line. Perhaps the final insult, in the light of the vaguely sexual flirtatiousness of the Whites during the mass, is the fact that the policing of the Blacks is even extended to segregating the men from the women. If religious activity in general can be seen as one of the chief means of ensuring that the Blacks adhere to an ideology favourable to colonial values, the mass at Dangan offers a clear concrete example of a religious event whose function is to reinforce the systems of control and discipline that are applied to the indigenous population. In the process, it further underlines the tendency on the part of the colonial masters to insist that the Blacks 'do as they say' rather than 'do as they do', which is a source of so much of the novel's ironic effect.

The mass at Dangan is a cleverly orchestrated piece of writing which draws on a range of comic effects to make an essentially serious set of observations about the nature of colonial relations. I shall examine the narrative and rhetorical strategies Oyono employs later in this study and for the time being would like to focus on the way the critique constantly deploys a lighter comedy of social manners in order to illustrate and emphasise far more serious issues. The case Oyono builds in order to attack colonialism does not rest on any appeal to moral, ethical or philosophical abstractions such as justice or equality. Instead he favours an inductive method which draws on a detailed observation of the empirical data provided by the behaviour of the Whites in order to demonstrate the general principles which actually operate in the colonial setting. This is why Toundi's role as observer situated within the enemy camp is so important. From this privileged position, first as *boy* to Père Gilbert and later to the Commandant, Toundi's apparently indiscriminate accounts of what he sees and hears gradually builds up a picture of individual and social behaviour patterns which in turn provide the evidence for an indictment of a whole system of social and political relations.

Toundi's observations thus allow the reader to draw a number of conclusions about the Whites and foremost among these is the fact that their behaviour is frequently hypocritical and duplicitous. Many further examples can be added to those already provided by the account of the mass at Dangan. There is, for instance, the purportedly common practice among the Whites of taking a black mistress while refusing to acknowledge this fact publicly. The mistress of the agricultural engineer, Sophie, complains to Toundi of this blatant show of double standards on the part of her lover: 'je suis fatiguée d'entendre: 'Sophie, ne viens pas aujourd'hui, un Blanc viendra me voir à la maison', 'Sophie, reviens, le Blanc est parti', 'Sophie, quand tu me vois avec une madame, ne me regarde pas, ne me salue pas', etc.' (*1*, pp.42–43). What makes such a situation all the more ridiculous is the fact that no one is fooled by these attempts at secrecy. The would-be deceiver and the not-quite-deceived are in effect colluding in a general system of hypocritical pretence, designed to maintain appearances. But the appearances they are so desperate to maintain involve the larger pretence that a whole edifice of discriminatory and segregationist practices are in some way justified.

Another example of the Whites' propensity to deceive themselves and each other is, of course, the affair between Madame, the Commandant's wife, and M. Moreau. Madame's marital infidelity is perhaps significant on a personal level as yet another example of deception among the Whites, but it is far more significant as a pointer to the general moral bankruptcy of the colonisers as a group. Indeed, the use of the form of address 'Madame', rather than a name, to refer to the character in question serves to depersonalise and generalise her so that she comes to represent a stock type, in much the same way that the Commandant himself can be seen as typical and representative of all *Commandants de cercle*. But the moral bankruptcy referred to is not merely a matter of the Whites failing to live up to standards they have set themselves. This would simply be an all too common human failing. It is rather a question of their seeking to proclaim the moral, ethical and cultural superiority of their own systems, and wishing to impose these on others, while simultaneously proving themselves incapable or unwilling to practice what they preach. There is in fact a constant discrepancy between, on the one hand, the unspoken official discourses (justifications for colonial policy, rationales for aspects of colonial governance, the moral and doctrinal teachings of the Christian missionaries) which are not expressed in the text but which haunt the novel as the implicit grounds for the colonial presence, and, on the other, the unofficial discourse of daily intercourse with the Blacks, through which the Whites express the realities of the colonial mind-set.

The most striking characteristic of the colonisers' attitude to the Blacks is the tendency to judge them by reference to preconceived notions and stereotypes which frequently fly in the face of empirical evidence. This vein is tapped whenever the Whites gather together socially, as for example, on the occasion of the reception at the Commandant's Résidence (*1*, pp.75–83). During the course of this short scene Blacks in general are subjected to a string of criticisms and pejorative commentary. Indeed the Whites appear to have few other subjects of conversation and they return to this pet topic with the regularity of a metronome. Toundi reports: 'On en revint aux nègres' (*1*, p.82); 'On reparla des nègres' (*1*, p.83), and the Blacks are always portrayed as constituting a threat to civilisation itself: 'Qu'allait devenir la civilisation?' (*1*, p.83). The actual content of this criticism is quite revealing, however. The first reproach levelled against the Blacks is their supposedly insatiable craving for alcohol. This observation conflicts directly with the behaviour of the entire company, since the Whites themselves are indulging quite unrestrainedly, as evidenced by the fact that Toundi is kept so busy serving them drinks, the fit of hiccups from M. Janopoulos (*1*, p.78), and the swaying gait they adopt when they eventually leave the reception: 'Les Blancs vacillaient sur le plancher comme sur une peau de banane' (*1*, p.83). Other angles of attack adopted by the Whites include Mme Salvain's comment that her *boy* smells of alcohol and filth, and the comment from the Doctor's wife: 'Il n'y a pas de moralité dans ce pays' (*1*, p.79). The novel as a whole would seem to be an illustration of the absence of morality among the Whites while the rather more personal question of body odours can scarcely be considered a one-sided problem. Only a few pages earlier Toundi remarks on the distinctive smell emanating from the unwashed agricultural engineer and how it reminds him of the Commandant: 'Il sentit la viande crue avec des nuances indéfinissables. Cette odeur, je la sentais tous les matins à la Résidence' (*1*, p.71).

The evidence which systematically undermines each of the criticisms levelled by the Whites is not produced in any obvious or overt way. As usual, Toundi observes and reports without commenting or evaluating what he has seen. But Oyono nevertheless plants the evidence required to expose this mindless series of jibes, either within the context of the scene itself or in very close textual proximity to it. He also provides at least one dissident voice from within the White community itself, that of M. Salvain, the schoolteacher. In an earlier conversation with the Commandant, Salvain had distanced himself from the stock prejudices of the colonialist mentality by suggesting that there are no inherent differences between the intellectual capacities of Blacks and Whites: 'Les petits noirs sont aussi intelligents que nos petits' (*1*, p.50). During the reception he goes further and refuses to countenance the notion that the Blacks are any more lacking in morality than Parisians. The furious White reaction, led by M. Fernand, is perhaps even more revealing of the White mentality than their original criticism of the Blacks in that it flatly refuses to envisage any possibility that the Blacks should be considered as equals or even as real human beings. M. Fernand says to Salvain:

> vous menez une activité qui n'est pas digne d'un Français de France! Vous dressez les indigènes contre nous... Vous leur racontez qu'ils sont des hommes comme nous, comme s'ils n'avaient pas déjà assez de prétentions comme cela! (*1*, p.80)

In the event, M. Salvain's work is as close as the novel ever comes to describing a version of enlightened colonial activity and an attempt to honour the colonial 'contract' to which I referred earlier. His isolation from his compatriots is a way of accentuating the message that the majority of Whites share a common tendency to dehumanise the Blacks and this in turn would suggest that the notion any such contract exists as a foundation for colonial relations is nothing more than a convenient fiction to be invoked by the Whites as and when it suits them.

The tendency to stereotype, to reify and ultimately to dehumanise the Blacks is a constant feature of the behaviour of the Whites and is illustrated on numerous occasions throughout the novel. Equality is not only absent from the colonial relationship in real, practical terms, it is denied as a matter of principle, as Fernand's tirade against Salvain demonstrates. Of course such a 'principled' form of discrimination, practised on the basis of race or colour of skin, usually goes by the name of racism and Oyono's purpose is precisely to illustrate the deep-seated racism inherent in the everyday reality of colonial relationships. Ironically, as we have seen, it is the religious context of the mass at Dangan with the organised segregation of the congregation into a space for Blacks and a space for Whites, each with its own set of conditions and standards of comfort, that provides the clearest example of such discrimination. As in this particular case, it is often in the context of spatial organisation that the discriminatory tendency is most easily apparent. It goes without saying that the novel describes a 'quartier européen' and a 'quartier indigène' which are contiguous but quite

distinct (*1*, p.107), just as there is a corner of the cemetery reserved
for Whites alone (*1*, p.31) as though the differences separating
colonisers and colonised are so fundamental as to be incapable of
being overcome even by death itself. But discrimination is not at
work only where social space is seen to be organised. It is also
frequently illustrated on a more personal level through the way it
affects the lives of individuals. When Sophie accompanies the
agricultural engineer on the tour of duty in the bush she is obliged to
ride in the back of the vehicle alongside Toundi and to suffer the
physical pain and indignity of being thrown about as the pick-up
speeds over the rough terrain. She is not slow to make the
comparison between this disrespectful treatment she is receiving at
the hands of a lover who is too embarrassed to acknowledge her true
status, and the displays of courtesy with which the Whites treat their
own women:

> — Mon Dieu!... Mais qu'est-ce qu'elles ont et que je
> n'ai pas?...
> — Les bonnes manières de Blancs, si c'est seulement
> pour entre eux, merde alors! Mon derrière est aussi
> fragile que celui de leurs femmes qu'ils font monter dans
> la cabine... (*1*, p.60)

This example of a difference in treatment, as so many other
examples in the novel of the application of different sets of
standards where Blacks and Whites are concerned, is symptomatic
of the mind-set of the Whites. And the question Sophie asks
ultimately leads the reader to wonder what exactly are the values
which the Whites could claim to be seeking to transmit to the Blacks
as they go about their 'civilising mission'.

There are two further characteristics of the White colonial
mentality which Oyono's portrayal seeks to foreground. Firstly,
there is the tendency displayed by the Whites to limit their
relationship with the Blacks to purely functional parameters. Just as
the Whites in *Une vie de boy* appear to have difficulty in seeing the
Blacks as fully human, they also have difficulty in seeing them as

distinct individuals with an individual identity. There is no evidence in the novel of any attempt on their part to get to know the Blacks and in place of knowledge the Whites rely on the sort of stereotyping I have already mentioned and the strategy of reducing the individual to a mere function. This is clear from the interview Toundi has with the Commandant before being taken on as his *boy* (*1*, pp.33–34) and is succinctly summed up by the cook when he says to Toundi:

> — Toundi, tu ne connaîtras jamais ton métier de boy...
> Quand comprendras-tu donc que pour le Blanc, tu ne vis
> que par tes services et non par autre chose! Moi, je suis
> le cuisinier. Le Blanc ne me voit que grâce à son
> estomac... (*1*, pp.131–32)

A corollary of this functionalist attitude is the absence of any true reciprocity in the relationship between Blacks and Whites. The two groups never truly interact. They simply co-exist in two contiguous but separate worlds. Moreover, the Whites arrogate to themselves the role of agents and imagine themselves as possessing the right to act upon the Blacks, while these latter are assumed to be passive and to submit to the moulding influence of White agency. The fact that the language used to describe this attitude fits a sexual as well as a political paradigm may be noted in passing, but my chief concern here is to highlight the non-reciprocal nature of the colonial relationship. The Whites rule, administer, govern, teach, convert, employ and, as the occasion seems to them to demand, judge, punish and imprison the colonised population. They are the perennial grammatical subject of the various actions that are performed in the novel, while the Blacks are consistently the object of this activity. Just how non-reciprocal the relationship is may be understood from the fact that it is inconceivable to imagine the roles being reversed, even temporarily.

The reactions of the Blacks themselves to this state of affairs is essentially fatalistic and opportunistic. With no power to alter the situation, they are portrayed as having no alternative but to accept it, and they either express their discontent in trivial and even playful shows of opposition, as in the case of Ondua, the tom-tom player, and Akoma and Mengueme, the traditional chiefs of Dangan, or, like Sophie, await an opportunity to turn the tables on the Whites and extract from them whatever money or goods it is possible to take. It could be argued that all of these examples involve forms of dishonesty or self-serving vanity. Ondua mocks the Whites secure in the knowledge that they cannot understand the language he is using; the Chiefs play their games of ingratiation and dissimulation for their own purposes; and Sophie's opportunistic thieving clearly suggests a total insensitivity to moral codes. It might seem too grandiose a rationale for this behaviour to suggest that in a totally repressive system any means of countering the oppressors, of hindering them and demonstrating a refusal to take them seriously are ways of reasserting one's dignity and perhaps even one's freedom. Oyono himself offers no such rationale. He is content to restrict himself to mere observation. As is the case in his descriptions of the physical condition of his fellow Africans and of their habitat, his portrayal of their behaviour is far from idyllic or idealised. In his scheme of things, pre-colonial Africa was no Eden and the Blacks no noble savages. Colonialism did not destroy a paradise, it inaugurated a particular type of relationship which he shows to have a debilitating and corrupting effect upon Whites as well as Blacks.

Against this background, Toundi is rather an odd and in many ways unrepresentative figure. Unlike the majority of his compatriots, for example, Toundi the child genuinely admires his White masters and seeks to emulate them in the vain hope that he will one day become like them and share the same standards of living as those they enjoy. In his naivety, Toundi observes and describes examples of discrimination and exploitation but he does not recognise them as such for all that. Neither does he seem to recognise segregation for what it is, nor the functionalist attitudes of his masters or the non-reciprocal nature of their dealings with Blacks. Instead, and against all the evidence of his own observations, he continues to believe in the myth of White superiority and the illusion that colonialism can benefit people like himself, a member of the indigenous population — in short, he retains his faith in the empty promise of the colonial contract. On the other hand, it is precisely because Toundi has such a benevolent attitude to the Whites that his fate so vividly illustrates the discrepancy between the myth and the reality of colonial rule.

But Toundi is not imprisoned and beaten to the point of death as a direct consequence of his naïve faith in the Whites. His problems derive from the other key aspect of his character: his role as observer. It would, however, be equally erroneous to conclude that his mistreatment is a result of his simply having seen too much of the intimate life of the Whites. The same could be said of the cook, the guard or of Baklu, the washman. Toundi's real difficulties arise from the fact that he fails to conform to the stereotype of the Black servant, and his position as observer is therefore perceived in a very different way by his masters. Indeed, Toundi is considered by Blacks and Whites alike to be fundamentally different and as belonging to neither of the two worlds he might be expected to inhabit. Not only can he read and write, he has aspirations to rise above his condition and enjoy the life style of his masters. At various points in the novel, his compatriots warn him of the dangers he is running in entertaining such illusory ideas about his own station. Baklu expresses it in typically African imagery: 'Toundi, mon frère... Que cherches-tu au juste? Depuis quand le pot de terre se frotte-t-il contre les gourdins? Que veux-tu donc?' (*1*, p.98) while the cook (*1*, pp.132–33) and Kalisia (*1*, pp.151–52) are more direct in their attempts to put him on his guard. For the Whites, Toundi's ambitions are also the key to his essential difference and Madame remarks upon it shortly after her arrival at the Résidence:

> — Tu donnes l'impression d'accomplir une corvée. Bien sûr, nous sommes contents de toi. Tu es irréprochable... Tu es toujours à l'heure, tu accomplis ton travail avec conscience... Seulement, tu n'as pas cette joie de vivre qu'ont tous les travailleurs

indigènes... On dirait que tu es boy en attendant autre chose. (*1*, p.86)

As this impression is gradually confirmed, Madame adopts the habit of referring to him mockingly as 'Monsieur Toundi'. The ironic tone of politeness and the ironic conferring of status are pointers to the fact that Toundi's ambitions unavoidably imply the possibility of an egalitarianism which constitutes a challenge to the very basis of colonial society. The use of the expression 'Monsieur Toundi' also indicates that Toundi is at last being individualised in a non-functional way and that he is being granted, however ironically, at least a hypothetical equality. For his compatriots these are so many proofs of the danger of his position. His naïvety appears to be synonymous with a failure to recognise and accept his allotted place within the structures of the colonial relationship as I have identified them.

This is not to say that the importance of Toundi's role as observer is in any way diminished. On the contrary, *Une vie de boy* makes such frequent references to acts of seeing and to different types of eye contact that any reading of the novel cannot fail but take them into account. And rather than examine Toundi's role as observer in isolation it is perhaps more important to consider how it fits into a wider system of references to the visual act which may in turn reinforce much that has already been said about colonial relationships.

Perhaps what best distinguishes the gaze of the Whites is what it fails to see rather than what it succeeds in seeing. Toundi remarks at one point, 'Les Blancs sont autant percés à nu par les gens du quartier indigène qu'ils sont aveugles sur tout ce qui se passe' (*1*, p.107). This blindness has a double significance since it alludes both to the Whites' hypocritical refusal to acknowledge their own failings (in this instance the extra-marital liaison between Madame and Moreau) as well as to their totally indifferent and therefore undifferentiating way of viewing the Blacks. This inability to differentiate visually between Blacks is another example of their failure to individualise them in any meaningful way, and Toundi offers a clear example of this process early on in the novel. Significantly, it is a common pastime for the young Blacks to treat the Whites as a form of spectacle but when M. Janopoulos sets his dog on the boys, it is the Commandant's failure to recognise his own servant that is possibly more shocking than the Greek's brutality: 'Mon commandant riait avec eux. Il ne m'a pas reconnu. Comment aurait-il pu me reconnaître? Pour les Blancs, tous les nègres ont la même gueule…' (*1*, p.44).

As we have already seen, this failure to differentiate among the Blacks is closely associated with the functionalist attitude of the Whites. They do not see the person, only the function he or she fulfils. This blindness to their surroundings (and to their own failings) contrasts with the acuteness of the vision of the Blacks. Indeed, the Whites are constantly and repeatedly the object of scrutiny by the locals: the social gatherings at the *Cercle européen*, Madame's visit to the market and the various receptions at the Résidence are all cases in point. The principle of non-reciprocity I identified earlier is repeated in this context too: the Blacks frequently observe the Whites and see them as an object of interest whereas the opposite is never the case.

On the other hand, once the nature of the observation changes, once the gaze has a different purpose, the principle of non-reciprocity is maintained but the roles are reversed. On the occasions when it is a question of imposing discipline, inflicting punishment or giving vent to cruelty or anger, the Whites seem to take pleasure in fixing their gaze on the chosen object. Indeed the Commandant's nickname is 'Zeuil-de-Panthère', presumably because of the cruelty of his gaze. There are numerous examples of Toundi in particular being subjected to this type of close scrutiny by his masters: when he is first interviewed by the Commandant ('Il plongea ses yeux dans les miens […] il me pénétra de son regard de panthère […]. Il […] me toisa de nouveau': *1*, pp.34–35); when he accidentally drops his cap on the floor ('je vis ses yeux devenir aussi petits que ceux d'un chat au soleil […]. Le commandant […] plongea ses yeux dans les miens': *1*, pp.36–37); when he explains to Madame that the Blacks in the market find her beautiful ('Ses yeux s'étaient rapetissés dans une expression indéfinissable': *1*, p.86) and when Madame is angry with him ('Ses yeux devinrent tout petits [...]. Elle me regarda, interdite': *1*, p.110). But of course, the Blacks have no corresponding gaze for the Whites and, at such moments, they must not reciprocate. They must lower their eyes and seek to make themselves not only invisible but unseeing.

What emerges from this rather complex network of instances of seeing and blindness, of visibility and invisibility, is a fairly simple principle. The Whites have the right to see but not be seen, whereas the Blacks, even if they see, must act as though they have seen nothing, or at least as though they have not understood what they have seen. The repressiveness of the colonial relationship is thus mirrored in the economy of visual activity as presented in the novel. And it is within this economy of visual activity that Toundi's role as observer must be placed if its particularities are to be fully appreciated. In the early part of the novel Toundi's observations, however significant they may be, are relatively simple and straightforward acts of seeing and reporting. At least they appear uncomplicated because Toundi himself does not appear to understand what he is observing. As the novel progresses, however, there is a far greater sense that Toundi's role is that of witness to a misdemeanour (or crime) or even that of spy in the enemy camp. This is certainly the case as the liaison between Madame and Moreau develops and Toundi furtively sneaks a glimpse of their kissing: 'Je [...] revins furtivement regarder par la fente de la fenêtre du salon d'où filtrait la lumière. M. Moreau embrassait Madame sur la bouche' (*1*, p.102). Likewise, on the return of the Commandant, Toundi is curious to see how Madame will react in a situation requiring duplicity: 'Il fallait que je voie les manières de Madame au retour de son mari, maintenant qu'elle l'avait trompé' (*1*, p.103).

In behaving thus, Toundi is of course breaking the rules of the colonial relationship as I have identified them above. He is not only daring to scrutinise his masters, he is remaining clearly visible as he does so. As narrator he bears witness to the hypocrisy and bad faith of the colonialists and their régime but as character he is literally a witness of certain particular events whose import he has clearly understood and which he is seen by Madame, Moreau and the Commandant to have understood. It is this combination of seeing and understanding which is unacceptable to the Whites, as Kalisia points out: 'Tant que tu seras là, le commandant ne pourra oublier [...]. Pour lui tu seras... je ne sais comment appeler ça... tu seras quelque chose comme l'œil du sorcier, qui voit et qui sait' (*1*, p.152). It is particularly unacceptable because it represents a threat to the very principles on which the colonial relationship operates. Toundi cannot be allowed to judge his masters as Kalisia again explains: 'malgré eux ils se sentent jugés par toi... Ils ne peuvent admettre ça...' (*1*, pp.152–53).

Hence it is not simply Toundi's role as observer which is instrumental in his downfall. It is the fact that his refusal to merge into the crowd, to accept the lot of the colonial subject and remain invisible, makes him recognisable for the Whites as a person who is capable of placing what he sees into a particular framework, having opinions about it and even arriving at judgements on it. Toundi's very presence in the latter stages of the novel obliges them to see themselves as they are seen by him and through his eyes.[5]

In considering the fate which Toundi suffers as a result of his inability to play the game required of him, it would be tempting to conclude that a recourse to violence is the ultimate sanction available to the Whites. But in fact, far from being a last resort, violence is a constant feature of the colonial relationship as described by Oyono. There is such an abundance of examples of gratuitous brutality, cruelty and violence that it is impossible to disentangle physical maltreatment, very often associated with what seems like sadistic

---

[5] The reference to seeing and being seen is one which Sartre uses to great effect in his essay *Orphée Noir*, where he writes of the first examples of African literary production in the following terms: 'Ces têtes que nos pères avaient courbées jusqu'à terre par la force, pensiez-vous, quand elles se relèveraient, lire l'adoration dans leurs yeux? Voici des hommes debout qui nous regardent et je vous souhaite de ressentir comme moi le saisissement d'être vus' (*15*, p.229).

pleasure, from any other aspect of the colonial enterprise.[6] The first
page of Toundi's journal alludes to the kick he receives from Père
Gilbert and this inaugurates a series of kicks (*1*, pp. 37 and 154),
crushed fingers (*1*, pp. 46 and 155) and general harrassment which
culminates in his imprisonment and torture in Moreau's prison.
Alongside these first-hand experiences of brutality, Toundi is also a
witness to the sufferings of his compatriots, ranging from the
systematic mistreatment of his parishioners by Père Vandermayer (*1*,
p.25) to the horrific beating inflicted on two Blacks at the orders of
Moreau but in the presence and to the great amusement of
Janopoulos (*1*, pp.114–15). The account of this latter incident
provides the clearest example of an attempt by Toundi to offer a
critical commentary on the events he has observed. In this instance
he explicitly links the ostensibly Christian rationale for the colonial
presence with the violent reality of the colonial relationship:

> On ne peut avoir vu ce que j'ai vu sans trembler. C'était
> terrible. Je pense à tous ces prêtres, ces pasteurs, tous ces
> Blancs qui veulent sauver nos âmes et qui nous prêchent
> l'amour du prochain. Le prochain du Blanc n'est-il que
> son congénère? Je me demande, devant de pareilles
> atrocités, qui peut être assez sot pour croire encore à tous
> les boniments qu'on nous débite à l'Eglise et au
> Temple... (*1*, p.115)

This scene is almost a prefiguring of the fate which will await
Toundi himself and affords him an opportunity to draw the
conclusions he will not be at leisure to draw later.

---

[6] In his own study of the novel, Jacques Chevrier considers the violence so
frequently a feature of colonial relations, in terms of 'conduites névrotiques',
and he goes on to write: 'A cet égard, *Une vie de boy* constitue un
témoignage consternant de la déshumanisation à laquelle aboutit une relation
de type sado-masochiste.' (*17*, p.44)

*Le Vieux Nègre et la médaille*

Many of the key features I have identified as characteristic of the colonial relationship described by Oyono in *Une vie de boy* are also present in *Le Vieux Nègre et la médaille*. The relations between Blacks and Whites in this second novel are grounded in the same political, social and economic conditions as are found in *Une vie de boy*, and it would be surprising if Oyono's second portrayal of colonial life did not present largely similar traits to the first. Any reading of the novel must take account of the way it highlights the enormous disparity between, on the one hand, the implicit rationale behind, and justification for, the colonial presence, based essentially on Enlightenment humanitarian values, and, on the other, the harsh realities of everyday life in the colonies as experienced by the indigenous population. In other words *Le Vieux Nègre et la médaille*, like *Une vie de boy*, speaks to readers of broken promises and unfulfilled contracts. Also like the earlier novel, it too, naturally, makes allusion to the discriminatory, hierarchical nature of colonial society, to the tendency on the part of Whites to dehumanise the Blacks and to reduce them to passive, functional roles, to the absence of any true reciprocity or interaction between the two groups and to the frequent recourse to violence, not as an ultimate sanction or an exceptional measure designed to solve a specific problem but as a banal and omnipresent accompaniment to every aspect of colonial life.

If there are many similarities between the two novels insofar as the portrayal of colonial relations is concerned, there are also, however, a number of significant differences. Perhaps, above all, *Le Vieux Nègre et la médaille* marks a change of perspective in that, in this second novel, Oyono focuses his attention far more on his fellow Africans than on the Whites. Whereas Toundi's journal recounts life at the Commandant's Résidence, at the very heart of White society, *Le Vieux Nègre et la médaille* offers a wider variety of settings among which African villages and scenes in the bush tend to have far greater prominence and the European quarter at Doum is merely a place to be visited briefly, usually at one's peril. Similarly, Oyono presents a wider variety of African characters in this second novel and there is a clearer attempt to provide them with individual physical and psychological characteristics than was the case in *Une vie de boy*. On this occasion, it is the White masters who tend to lumped together *en masse* and treated as a homogeneous, undifferentiated entity with little psychological substance. Oyono's treatment of character and setting would both seem to authorise the conclusion therefore that *Le Vieux Nègre et la médaille* is far more concerned with the African experience of the colonial relationship than with a further attempt to analyse its constituent elements.

Nevertheless, if there is one area of colonial life which seems to stand out as a target for particular attack in the second novel it is the activity of the missionaries, represented in this instance primarily by Père Vandermayer. This is not to say that Oyono ever attacks Christianity on a doctrinal level by questioning the validity of its teachings from a spiritual, philosophical or ethical point of view. Such concerns have no place in his writings. On the other hand, where Oyono is probably at his most trenchantly satirical, as Mongo Beti is in *Le Pauvre Christ de Bomba* (1956), is in his portrayal of the way missionaries collude and collaborate with the secular arms of colonial government and relegate their own supposedly spiritual interests to a place of secondary importance behind the military, commercial and political interests of other colonial agents, thus effectively sabotaging their own mission and abdicating any serious claim to moral authority. Rather than acting as a check on the material interests driving the administrators, soldiers, politicians and merchants by an appeal to spiritual values, the missionaries' role, as described by Oyono, would appear to be to strengthen the authority of these colleagues by suggesting that civil law is somehow synonymous with the will of God. Thus their intervention into the lives of the Blacks more often than not acts to reinforce the control mechanisms of the secular colonial state. While the secular authorities insist on the physical subservence of the Blacks, the missionaries appear intent on enslaving their hearts and minds through various forms of mythopœic manipulation.

At the outset of *Le Vieux Nègre et la médaille* the protagonist, Meka, would appear to be a singularly successful example of the work of the missionaries in these respects. Whatever Meka's feelings about the Whites in general, as a convert to Christianity he identifies closely with the religious message the missionaries convey. Unfortunately he is not particularly adept at making any clear distinction between the spiritual teachings of the Church and attempts by its representatives to further its material interests. The passage describing the way he has sacrificed his land to the missionaries indicates the extent of his gullibility in this respect:

> Il avait 'donné' ses terres aux prêtres et habitait une petite case misérable au village dont la mission portait le nom et qui s'étendait au pied du cimetière chrétien. Il avait eu la grâce insigne d'être le propriétaire d'une terre qui, un beau matin, plut au Bon Dieu. Ce fut un père blanc qui lui révéla sa divine destinée. Comment pouvait-on aller contre la volonté de Celui-qui-donne? [...]. Il suivit, enthousiaste, l'édification du quartier du seigneur sur la terre de ses ancêtres. (2, p.16)

It would seem therefore that if Meka is considered an exemplary Christian it is because he serves the material interests of the missionaries rather than for any specifically religious reason. Certainly Meka, like Toundi before him, is a willing colonial subject who, far from resisting the colonial presence, actually appears to embrace it with open arms. But whereas Toundi's espousal of the colonialist enterprise was motivated by greed and an appetite for the material benefits he hoped to enjoy, Meka's enlistment into the cause of the colonialists is specifically linked to ideological factors. In this respect *Le Vieux Nègre et la médaille* complements *Une vie de boy* just as Meka the idealist complements Toundi the materialist. Whatever the individual motivations which might lead Blacks to place their trust in the promises held out by the colonialists, Oyono demonstrates that they are doomed to disappointment.

The complicity between the spiritual authority of the missionaries and the secular authority of the civil administration is further illustrated in the attitude displayed by the Whites to the distillation of *arki*, the preferred alcoholic drink of many locals, including Meka. Although the administration has banned its production and consumption for purely commercial reasons and in order to skew the market in favour of French-produced wine and liqueurs, the Blacks continue to drink their own brew in defiance of the law. When legal prohibition has only a limited effect, the police chief, Gosier d'Oiseau, colludes with the priest, Père Vandermayer, to ensure that the message goes out that drinking *arki* is a sinful as well as an illegal act:

> Gosier d'Oiseau s'en était remis au Révérend Père Vandermayer. Le missionnaire, du haut de sa chaire, avait eu vite fait de condamner cette boisson qui, disait-il, noircissait les dents de l'âme de ses paroissiens. Il avait décrété que tous ceux des chrétiens qui en buvaient commettaient un péché mortel en avalant chaque gorgée.
> (*2*, p.16)

Thus the commercial interests of the colonialists are defended by an alliance between an arbitrary legal and judicial system and the compliant spiritual authority of the missionaries.

A similar confusion of values and authority is also discernible in the event which lies at the very heart of the novel: the decision to honour Meka by bestowing a medal upon him. Is the medal intended to commemorate an action or an event which took place in the religious or the secular domain? Is it conferred in recognition of Meka's spiritual or civic worthiness? Is it, in fact, a civil honour or a religious award? The fact that the medal is to be presented at a ceremony on the occasion of the *fête nationale*, on the 14th July, by the 'chef des Blancs' would suggest that the affair involves a civic award. Yet what distinguishes Meka from his compatriots and singles him out for the award is the fact that he was willing to allow himself to be expropriated so that the Christian mission could be built. Whether the award is religious or civil remains pointedly blurred: the very confusion as to its nature illustrates the harmony of purpose behind the secular and the religious arms of the colonial régime. Moreover, other references to medals in the novel appear to link them with religious beliefs of one sort or another and foster a further blurring of boundaries. Firstly there is a description of Christians returning from mass as: 'ces êtres constellés de médailles, de scapulaires, de chapelets et parfois d'une puissante croix de plomb suspendue à leur cou' (2, p.35), and secondly, when Meka fears for his life as the *Foyer africain* collapses around his ears, he seeks to reassure himself that St Christopher is protecting him: 'Il explora son cou pour voir s'il portait encore sa médaille saint Christophe [...]. Meka réalisa enfin [...] que la baraque allait s'écrouler sur lui. Mais il ne s'affola plus, ce bon saint Christophe était avec lui' (2, pp.132–33). On the one hand, these references serve to blur distinctions between Christianity and animistic practices since both contain a strong element of superstitious belief. But they also help to explain the context within which many of the Blacks see the Commandant's decision to honour Meka with a medal. The event has a quasi-religious significance for them and marks an almost mystical association of Meka with the power of the colonial régime. It is for this reason that family, friends and acquaintances of Meka feel that in some vague and ill-defined way they are moving closer within the ambit of power and that their communities will benefit from improved infrastructure and better services as a result of Meka's new status.

This interpretation of the significance of the medal is simply one among several that the novel proposes. It is, of course, an essentially metonymic view of the medal's significance in that it implies a sense that the medal's power radiates outwards touching most deeply those in closest proximity and contiguity to it. This view is best illustrated by the words of Nkolo who brings news of Meka's good fortune to his brother-in-law, Engamba:

> Ta famille, tes amis, les amis de tes amis seront désormais des privilégiés. Il leur suffira de dire: 'Je suis

> l'ami de l'ami du beau-frère de Meka' pour que toutes
> les portes leur soient ouvertes. Moi-même qui vous
> parle, je me sens un peu décoré... (*2*, p.42)

Similarly, Meka's wife, Kelara, is rather comically assumed to have
become a White by virtue of her very proximity to the honour her
husband is to receive: 'Maintenant que son mari va recevoir une
médaille, elle deviendra une femme blanche' (*2*, p.42).

To this metonymic interpretation of the medal's significance
can be added a metaphoric view according to which the medal is
seen as a symbol of a renewal of the relationship existing between
Blacks and Whites. Expressed in its least ambitious terms, this would
treat the medal as a sign of a renewed friendship, which is the rather
noncommittal way the Whites refer to it. But expressed more
ambitiously, this view sees the medal as a symbol of the possibility
of a wholesale renegotiation of the colonial relationship in which the
Whites finally abandon empty rhetoric and replace words with deeds.
Naively and optimistically the bestowal of the medal is taken as a
sign that the liberty, equality and fraternity of Republican rhetoric
and the injunction to love one's fellow man which is at the heart of
the Christian message conveyed by the missionaries, might finally be
translated into some new form of colonial dispensation. Oyono
illustrates the contrast between rhetoric and action in the most direct
way possible by having Meka, through the services of an interpreter,
respond to a speech by inviting 'le grand Chef' to share a meal with
him:

> — Meka demande si vous pouvez venir manger avec lui
> le bouc que son beau-frère lui a apporté pour célébrer la
> médaille que vous lui avez donnée. Il le dit parce que
> depuis que les Blancs sont ici, il n'a jamais vu un Blanc
> inviter un indigène ni un indigène inviter un Blanc.
> Etant donné qu'ils sont maintenant des amis ou plus que
> cela comme le grand Chef l'a dit, il faut bien que
> quelqu'un commence. (*2*, p.119)

The politeness and the vacuous nature of the White's response: 'Il mange ton bouc en pensée et pleure de ne pouvoir venir le manger avec toi dans ta case' (2, p.120), and especially the issuing of yet another vague, procrastinating promise: 'il t'invite à manger avec lui pour une autre fois. Et cette promesse est le commencement d'une saison nouvelle... quelque chose comme ça...' (2, p.120) are clear indications that nothing has changed and that empty promises are the very substance of the colonial relationship. The interpreter's dismissive, rather offhand attitude as to the accuracy of the message he is asked to convey only serves to emphasise the fact that the content cannot be taken seriously.

The way events turn out merely confirms what readers have known all along, namely, that there is a far less flattering interpretation of the Whites' decision to honour Meka than the majority of the Blacks care to acknowledge. The medal has little intrinsic value and is therefore an inexpensive way of appearing to reward Meka for his services to the colonial powers. It is, in fact, a way of fobbing him off. As events surrounding and following the ceremony unfold they lend ever increasing weight to this view. And once this interpretation is accepted, firstly by Kelara, who hears a voice in the crowd crudely express the truth about Meka's situation: '— Moi, je dis qu'on aurait mieux fait de l'habiller de médailles! [...]. Il a bien perdu ses terres et ses fils pour ça...' (2, p.105) and eventually by Meka himself, not only is the medal stripped of any symbolic value but those things of which it was a symbol: friendship between Blacks and Whites, collaboration in a spirit of solidarity and fraternity, an opening of channels of communication, expressions of mutual respect, all are seen as illusions and mere displays of the rhetoric on which the edifice of colonial relationships continues to be founded.

There is no real sense of surprise when the illusions and false hopes engendered by the award of the medal are eventually shattered. This is because the novel always allows a realistic evaluation of the true nature of colonial life to be made in parallel with the naively optimistic discourse Oyono purposely develops. Meka's own experience provides enough empirical evidence to demonstrate that he and his entourage are being naïve when they consider the award of the medal to represent a new beginning rather than another empty ritual. This evidence includes, for example, the miserable living conditions of Meka and Kelara as well as of their compatriots in villages such as Zourian and Nkongo. Moreover the summons to appear before the Commandant in the opening pages of the novel fills Meka with trepidation. He has learned from experience that contact with the Whites is dangerous and to be avoided whenever possible. Thus, at the same time as Oyono describes the hopes that a new era is dawning in colonial relations, he ensures that the text also presents a more realistic, down-to-earth and ultimately more accurate portrait of those relations.

The reality is of course that Blacks and Whites inhabit two separate but contiguous universes. They exist side by side but never really come into contact. One of the promises contained in the award of the medal to Meka is that some form of interaction will take place between the two worlds and some form of contact will be made. In the event, no such contact or interaction happens. As the ceremony itself demonstrates, Meka is made to stand inside a chalk circle under a blazing sun, isolated in time and space as he awaits the arrival of 'le grand chef des Blancs', cut off from his compatriots as much as from the Whites who are sheltering in the shade. And Meka's position 'dans un cercle de chaux, entre deux mondes, le sien et celui de ceux qu'on avait d'abord appelés les 'fantômes' quand ils étaient arrivés au pays' (*2*, p.96) leads him to an almost existential form of doubt about his predicament: 'Lui, il ne se trouvait ni avec les siens ni avec les autres. Il se demanda ce qu'il faisait là' (*2*, p.96). Only gradually do these first inklings of doubt become confirmed as Meka, lost in the storm in the European quarter at night, is arrested, beaten and imprisoned for having literally ventured into the world of the Whites. The fact that this is precisely what the award of the medal seemed to be inviting him to do is not recognised by the men who arrest him.

But Meka's adventure involves many other examples of both successful and unsuccessful attempts at recognition. The award of the medal itself must be read as a form of recognition by the Whites of Meka's support for them. But this is only superficially the case since everything about this honour, especially the ceremony and the reception at the *Foyer africain* which follows it, smacks of tokenism. The Whites are paying lip service to the concept of gratitude rather than expressing real gratitude to an individual. At the presentation ceremony, for example, far from showing concern for the physical comfort and well-being of an honoured guest, well advanced in years, they put Meka on show and make a spectacle of him. His own sense of alienation and isolation is indeed quite an adequate symbolic representation of the plight of all colonial subjects in their dealings with their masters. He is treated not as a human being made of flesh and blood with identifiable physical needs but as a dehumanised symbol. So an event which supposedly has its origins in an act of recognition quickly takes on a different meaning and comes to signify something closely akin to its opposite. The Whites are involved in an act of non-recognition as they fail to recognise their common humanity with Meka and choose instead to make use of him for their own purposes. This is nowhere more clearly illustrated than in the way Oyono describes the Whites closing ranks to exclude Meka from their circle immediately after the award: 'Meka ne sut comment il s'était retrouvé à l'extérieur du cercle que les Blancs avaient formé autour de leur grand Chef' (*2*. p.107). And it is, of course, left to the missionary most indebted to Meka, Père Vandermayer, angrily to refuse any contact with him and thus underline the real indifference the Whites feel towards him: 'Il alla tapoter l'épaule du Père Vandermayer, qui le fusilla du regard tout en l'écartant d'un mouvement violent du revers de la main' (*2*, pp.107–08).

If events at the ceremony and at the reception seem to suggest that the Whites' recognition of Meka's services counts as no real recognition at all, then the events that follow these scenes make it abundantly clear that this is the case since they hinge on the policemen's failure to recognise Meka's story as true or to identify Meka himself. This failure to recognise Meka is repeated the following day when he appears before Gosier d'Oiseau after a night spent in prison. The individual singled out by the authorities as the exemplary colonial subject, the one selected by them to receive an unprecedented honour, has in a matter of hours once again merged into the crowd and has become virtually unrecognisable. These are uncomfortable realities which illustrate the truth of the colonial relationship. Oyono's narrative demonstrates that, as far as the Whites are concerned, the award of the medal involves a masquerade of recognition which cloaks an inherent failure on their part to recognise the common humanity of the Blacks.

For Kelara and Meka the process is reversed. When they understand that the award of the medal is merely an empty gesture, that it is not an act of recognition but quite the contrary, then they experience a moment of illumination as to the true nature of their situation as colonial subjects. Their own original failure to recognise the truth about themselves gives way to a deeper kind of recognition. For Kelara, this happens when the mocking voice in the crowd at the presentation ceremony reveals to her the extent to which she and her husband have been duped by the Whites. Meka, on the other hand, clings to his illusions until the moment after his arrest when he realises that Gosier d'Oiseau does not know who he is. The White's failure to recognise him forces Meka to recognise the truth about his own situation and his own status in the eyes of the Whites. He explains to the interpreter: 'Puisqu'il me demande qui je suis, dis-lui que je suis le dernier des imbéciles, qui hier croyait encore à l'amitié des Blancs...' (2, p.150).

In the case of Meka, the moment of recognition is not limited to a simple realisation that his past actions have been naïve. It has been prepared by various moments when Meka has entertained questions as to his own true identity and has hesitatingly sought to re-evaluate his own intrinsic status and worth but this time in an exclusively African context. At the ceremony itself, which ironically marks the point at which Meka is most clearly acting as a stooge of the colonial administration, it is his sense of family and tribal honour which helps him to find the courage to bear the physical pain he is made to endure:

> Enfin quoi! se dit-il, je suis un homme! Mes ancêtres
> m'ont laissé tel quel! Ils doivent me voir dans cet
> endroit où je me trouve... N'essayons pas de leur faire
> honte. J'ai été circoncis au couteau et le sorcier a craché
> du piment sur ma blessure. Je n'ai pas pleuré... (*2*, p.
> 97)

And later, after suffering the ignominy of physical abuse at the hands
of the guards who have arrested him, he tries to make sense of what
is happening through reference to ancestral family and tribal values:

> Comment lui, le descendant des grands Meka, 'les
> Souches-immuables-sous l'orage', les 'Rivières-qui-
> n'ont-pas-peur-de-la-forêt', les 'Serpents-pythons', les
> 'Rocs', les 'Fromagers', les 'Elé-phants', les 'Lions', le
> fils de ceux-là mêmes qui n'avaient jamais ployé sous la
> force d'un autre homme, lui qui avait le culte de l'amitié,
> comment pouvait-on le traiter ainsi? (*2*, p.145)

Finally, when summoned before Gosier d'Oiseau after his
night in the cells, Meka's attention wanders as he remembers the
days when the first Whites appeared in the country and the part his
ancestors had played in combating them. He concludes defiantly that
he is not afraid of the Whites and, perhaps more significantly, he
equates the day of his baptism into the Christian faith with the day he
entered slavery: '— Le jour où je suis devenu un esclave!' (*2*, p.152).
This series of reflections has a common thread in that they
each hark back to pre-colonial days when traditional African values
continued to provide a framework for interpersonal relationships.
The stress on personal bravery, group solidarity, communal inter-
dependence and the duty of hospitality to strangers which figure in
Meka's reflections are all echoed in the numerous scenes in the novel
which portray the Africans in everyday interaction. Such reflections
contrast starkly of course with Meka's behaviour in the period prior
to the ceremony when he is portrayed as making increasingly
ludicrous efforts at assimilation. The 'zazou' jacket and the new

shoes he buys are indicative of his efforts to force his African *persona* into ever closer conformity to a model which he believes will be more palatable to the Whites. The physical discomfort he experiences in trying to squeeze his feet into the shoes is suggestive of an existential discomfiture in the role he is attempting to play throughout the ceremony itself. The great play that Oyono makes of Meka's physical distress and alienation, at this point in the narrative, reinforces the sense that there is something fundamentally unnatural about Meka's docility and his readiness to accept every conceivable constraint in order to play the part of the exemplary colonial subject correctly.

Thus, if the moment of illumination which eventually arises from this suffering leads Meka finally to reject the role he has been playing, it is simultaneously the moment when he embraces his own African-ness. By the closing stages of the novel the various forms of mediation which the colonial presence had inflicted upon Meka's personality have been sloughed off, and the Meka who returns home to Kelara after his ordeal is portrayed as an authentic African rather than an unsuccessful attempt at assimilation to colonial values. Indeed, his return home is punctuated by a number of actions and events closely related to the natural environment and which have peculiar significance in terms of African customs and beliefs. As he progresses through the forest (*2*, pp.155–59) the flora and fauna he encounters are seen as rich with meanings and evocative of superstitious beliefs predating Christian evangelisation. So Meka's return home is also a symbolic return to his African origins and the Christian prayer he began to mouth at the outset of the journey is never completed as the veneer of Christian teaching is washed away by this immersion in the African bush: 'Toutes ces superstitions avaient rejailli dans son esprit, balayant comme un raz de marée des années d'enseignement et de pratiques chrétiens' (*2*, p.159).

The re-establishment of an African value system, which is presented in these pages as closely associated with the natural environment, is reiterated in a socio-cultural context once Meka arrives back at the village. African solidarity and communal values envelope Meka as he is welcomed home and, as Nti explains, the significance of Meka's personal experience is fully assumed by the whole group:

> — Si les larmes ne ressuscitent pas les morts, celles que nous avons versées ici ne sont pas inutiles... [...].
> — Je dis qu'elles n'auront pas été inutiles parce que ce qui est arrivé à l'homme mûr appelé Meka nous est arrivé à tous par lui...
> — A nous tous! A nous tous!
> Ces mots volèrent de bouche en bouche. (*2*, p.170)

Thus the closing sections of the novel depict a Meka who is not only in harmony with nature but also in harmony with his family, friends and acquaintances in the village. There is a resolution of sorts here but it is clearly only a partial one, since Meka is no more in a position to ignore the power of the colonial masters at the close of the novel than he was at the outset. But Meka's experiences (including his first-hand experience of the arbitrary and gratuitous recourse to physical violence which is once again shown to underpin colonial authority) lead him to a more lucid view as to the relative merits of the two worlds that he previously attempted to inhabit simultaneously. In particular, what Meka seems implicitly to have understood by the close of the novel is that the sorts of status that appear to be available to those who collude with colonialism pale into insignificance when compared to the sense of self-esteem that comes from remaining true to one's own cultural heritage and its value systems.

Both *Une vie de boy* and *Le Vieux Nègre et la médaille* have something of the *Bildungsroman* about them since both Toundi and Meka are involved in a voyage of self-discovery as they each in their different ways experience close contact with the colonial system. For each of them the contact is fraught with dangers, and the lessons they learn prove painful and even fatal. If Toundi is destroyed by the encounter whereas Meka survives, it is no doubt because Toundi, unlike Meka, fails to draw the conclusions that his experience offers as to the true nature of colonial relations. Both begin by believing that the Whites will keep the promises of the implicit colonial contract and both eventually are overwhelmed by the empirical evidence that the contrary is the case.

## 2. Rhetorical strategies

A question often asked in relation to literature emanating from erstwhile colonies, particularly of writers of the generation of Oyono who bridge the gap between the colonial era and the arrival of national independence, concerns the audience the writers had in mind when producing their work. The question is often couched in terms of a stark choice: are the writers primarily addressing a metropolitan audience or are they writing in the hope of communicating with their compatriots? Each of these broadbrush options carries with it a political agenda, of course. The writer who targets an essentially metropolitan readership could be seen as in some ways collaborating, at least on a cultural level, with the forces of oppression, whereas the writer whose chief concern is to speak to his compatriots, even through the medium of a 'foreign' language and non-indigenous cultural forms, can be more easily seen as seeking to resist oppression and as having a stronger claim to cultural authenticity, whatever that may mean. But there can, of course, be no simple answer to such a question, even if one accepts the implied premise that writers need to write *for* some putative and identifiable audience. Political agendas apart, what the question inevitably brings in its train is a debate involving many of the following elements: the economics of literary production and consumption, the prevailing market conditions in the literature-related industries, the high levels of illiteracy in many postcolonial societies, the relevance or irrelevance of metropolitan cultural forms to postcolonial cultures and the language barriers that hinder the diffusion of texts. Even when restricted to the writings of an individual author, such debates tend to be inconclusive and are probably more important for the issues they raise than for the light they actually shed on a writer's work.

No doubt a novelist like Oyono is writing first and foremost for a linguistic community (francophone in this instance) irrespective of the national, social or ethnic origins of the readers or of their political leanings. We might be better advised to see Oyono not so much as addressing an audience as seeking to influence the varied audiences that may chance upon his work. This would help us to think less in terms of messages and addressees and more in terms of open-ended rhetorical strategies through which he may be seen to be inviting all and any of his readers to adopt new and more critical perspectives on an all too familiar world.

This is not to say that the varied nature of his readership does not demand that he display a high degree of sensitivity to national, social, ethnic and political diversity. On the contrary, successful rhetoricians are those whose technique allows them to persuade followers of all camps to review their allegiances. Oyono's purpose in writing *Une vie de boy* and *Le Vieux Nègre et la médaille* was not so much to attack the abuses of the colonial régime he himself had experienced as to expose the internal contradictions of the whole colonial enterprise and in particular the hypocrisy and the moral and ethical duplicity of its representatives. It is easy to imagine how an outright attack upon, and a direct condemnation of, various forms of injustice might lead to a hardening of attitudes and a division into two opposing camps: the colonisers and the colonised. Instead, by refusing to denounce colonialism *per se*, and indeed by portraying in each novel protagonists who have largely espoused the cause of their colonial masters, Oyono is able to retain the sympathies and interest of a wider audience. Readers who may feel no antipathy whatsoever to colonialism as a phenomenon will not progress very far in a reading of either novel without recognising the deficiencies of the colonisers whom Oyono portrays and the evils that result from the skewed relationships which their régime institutionalises. Likewise, Oyono's often brutal portrayal of the squalid living conditions and miserable working circumstances of the Blacks, as well as their often unprepossessing physical appearance, clearly indicates that his vision of Africa, even the Africa that has barely been touched by the colonial presence, is far from being an idealised one. This is not an idyllic, sentimental portrait of Africa for European consumption, nor are the Blacks noble savages who have fallen victim to the colonial presence. They are portrayed as unfortunate human beings living in unfortunate circumstances. If we were to extrapolate from the portrait Oyono draws of them, we might say that they were in need of better conditions of hygiene, a greater level of instruction, and greater prosperity. But this is an extrapolation that Oyono himself never makes any more than Shakespeare suggests that Hamlet should cheer up.

## Narrative techniques and narrative structure

The portrait that Oyono offers then, makes considerable capital out of the ostensible objectivity of the two narrators, at least in so far as the description of physical details is concerned. Toundi and the third person narrator of *Le Vieux Nègre et la médaille* both share the same dispassionate eye for the unattractive, even comically shocking, detail. An example occurs early on in *Une vie de boy* when Toundi notes, 'J'avais un oncle que je n'aimais pas à cause de ses croûtes de gale. Sa femme sentait, comme lui, le poisson avarié' (*1*, p.19). In the case of Toundi's narration, such straightforward references to the unattractive features of characters makes the reader aware that this narrative voice will not shrink from telling unpleasant truths. At the same time, readers may feel a certain distance between their own views and the point of view of the young narrator. For example, they may not share his taste for decaying porcupine ('L'arôme du porc-épic que nous avions trouvé à moitié dévoré par les fourmis, pris depuis deux jours à l'un des pièges de mon père, me donnait de l'appétit': *1*, p.20) any more than they share his views on the munificence of Père Gilbert to whom he claims to owe everything (*1*, p.24). The combination of straight-forwardness and naivety in Toundi make him a reliable but evidently limited narrator. Toundi's naivety is of fundamental importance to Oyono's strategy here. More often than not he is quite content to observe and merely to note his observations without passing judgement on them. He thus collates and presents to the reader a mass of empirical evidence whose significance he himself shows little sign of understanding. And because this evidence calls out for a judgement to be made, the reader feels an ever-increasing urge to fill the void and provide the judgement that Toundi is apparently incapable of making. In this way, the onus of responsibility passes from the character to the reader: what counts is not Toundi's judgement of colonial society or the behaviour of the Whites but what the reader comes to think about these things.

Toundi's naivety is clearly an appropriate attribute for a small boy, and Oyono reaps the benefits that flow from such a narrative perspective. As is the case when faced with Montesquieu's *Lettres persanes*, European readers are suddenly obliged to see themselves through the eyes of the Other and make sense of themselves through discourse they no longer control. The diary form which the novel adopts produces a narrative made up of a series of loosely related *tableaux* presented in chronological order. This allows Oyono to offer a series of short scenes and thumb-nail sketches which only gradually develop a dramatic momentum as Toundi relates the account of Madame's liaison with M. Moreau. The increasingly novelistic tone of some of the *tableaux*, particularly in the second *cahier* (for example, *1*, p.165), may be in keeping with the idea of a narrator who is himself maturing in years, but it can equally well be seen as evidence of Oyono's less than complete mastery of the diary form he has chosen.

The decision to organise his narrative in the form of a diary written from an innocent perspective leaves Oyono with a dual challenge. Firstly, Toundi must remain naively uncritical for as long as possible if Oyono is to achieve maximum benefit from this strategy. In other words, Toundi must continue to recount his experiences while showing little propensity for learning from them. This is, of course, something of a struggle and it is tempting for readers to attempt to trace Toundi's personal growth into a more enlightened frame of mind as the novel progresses and to see his narratorial stance as being essentially an increasingly ironic one. The text offers little sustained or consistent justification for such a reading and Oyono's efforts seem rather to pull in the opposite direction and work towards maintaining his innocence for as long as possible. Such consistent naivety, flying in the face of all the evidence, requires perhaps an exceptional degree of suspension of disbelief on the part of the reader. The second challenge relates to the first in that Oyono must avoid allowing the focus of the novel to slip from being a critique of colonial society into a detailed account of Toundi's personal drama. The key to Oyono's response to both these challenges is the absence of psychological depth in any of the characters he portrays in *Une vie de boy*, but especially in Toundi. The characters are consistently observed from the outside and the motivations for their actions are never explored in any detail. Remarkably in a first person narration, this largely applies also to Toundi himself since the reader is rarely given any insight into Toundi's own thoughts and feelings. Toundi's inner growth and development have to be surmised from the events he recounts rather than from any analysis accompanying their narration, and his naivety seems to bubble up irrepressibly until the final stages of the novel when he is imprisoned and tortured.

A further difficulty facing Oyono is that of incorporating into his novel an account of the death of his own narrator. If this is manœuvred relatively easily by recourse to a paratextual account of Toundi's demise and the discovery of his diaries, which is placed at the opening of the novel, as Dorothy Blair has pointed out (7, p.223) there remains the difficulty of composing final entries in the diary which do not overly offend against verisimilitude given the torture to which Toundi has been subjected. The degree of implausibility can be measured at its maximum when Toundi, transferred from prison to hospital with a high fever, somehow manages to write his final entry. The opening paratext serves another purpose quite apart from seeking to resolve a practical narratorial problem. It introduces into the novel a second level of narration quite distinct from that constituted by Toundi's two *cahiers*. The paratext speaks to the reader from a different location in space and time and from a different perspective. It thus implies that Toundi's discourse has itself journeyed from a fictional space within which it risked being neatly contained and has emerged into a wider, albeit still fictional world, where its lessons can be understood and even corroborated by the experience of others. The first-person narrator of the paratext is moved by Toundi's questioning of the true status and identity of Blacks who have been subjected to French colonial rule: '*mon frère, que sommes-nous? Que sont tous les nègres qu'on dit français?*' (*1*, pp.12–13) and his response might well be the sort of response Oyono himself is seeking to elicit from his African readers: '*A vrai dire, dans ma juvénile insouciance, je ne m'étais jamais posé cette question. Je me sentis devenir stupide*' (*1*, p.13). In this respect, the relationship of the two *cahiers* to the paratext perhaps offers a model for the sort of journey the novel as a whole must undertake as it seeks to push its readers into a critical reassessment of colonialism and its effects. But of course all this precedes the reader's acquaintance with Toundi's story just as it also provides a chilling context within which to read it.

    *Le Vieux Nègre et la médaille* relies equally on the naivety of its protagonist as a key strategy in its efforts to expose the hypocrisy of the colonial system. But the fact that Meka is not the narrator of his own story means that the naivety is a feature of the narrative account itself and is not incorporated into the narrative act, as is the case in *Une vie de boy*. It clearly suits Oyono's purpose that Meka's illusions about the Whites should last as long as possible so that maximum effect can be achieved through prolonging the contrast between his illusions and the harsh reality of colonial rule. But whereas in *Une vie de boy*, the destruction of Toundi's illusions simultaneously involves Toundi's own destruction, and thereby the act of narration itself, in the second novel the narration can continue as smoothly as before even after Meka's illusions about the Whites are shattered.

    This possibly goes some way to accounting for the fact that both the techniques of narration and the narrative structure of *Le Vieux Nègre et la médaille* demonstrate a more polished, literary quality than are in evidence in the earlier novel. For one thing, Oyono does not need to imitate the rather unsophisticated language of a child as he does in *Une vie de boy*, particularly in the early stages. Instead a more self-confident narratorial tone is discernible from the very first chapter of *Le Vieux Nègre et la médaille*. Even within this chapter, which selectively recounts a day in the life of Meka, Oyono structures the narrative around a variety of settings as the scene switches from the *case* he shares with his wife, Kelara, to the drinking den run by Mami Titi, to the Commandant's residence in the White district of town and back to the *case* where the day's news is discussed by Meka's friends. The variety of spatial locations is matched by an equally dynamic use of temporal settings. The ostensible time frame of the narrative — the single day on which Meka goes into town in response to the Commandant's summons — is in fact exploded by, on the one hand, explanatory flashbacks providing the background which allows the reader to understand Meka's personality and history better, and, on the other, by anticipatory reflections on the forthcoming award of the medal. Ellipsis also plays a major role in this chapter in that what might well be considered the central event of this day, the encounter with the Commandant, is in fact elided in both spatial and temporal terms. It is suppressed in the actual chronology of the day in order to reappear as a pretext for narration(s) in Meka's *case* that evening. This 'relocation' of the event into a different narrative time and space ensures that it is incorporated into an African context in which African values are brought to bear upon it. It should be noted in passing that this foregrounding of the act of narration is entirely consonant with the African oral tradition. The event is no longer just an event in a narrative sequence, it is an object of narration which is presented and represented to an ever-changing audience as visitors to the *case* arrive and depart, and it is commented upon, discussed and evaluated. It thus reflects an oral tradition which places considerable importance not only on the set-piece oral delivery of tales and other narrative forms in an essentially participatory mode, but also on the importance of informal discussion and deliberation as a way of cementing social relations and ensuring the continuing cohesiveness of the group.

Within this context of oral African narrative practice it is not surprising that an event so important as the honour to be done to Meka is considered news of such magnitude that its telling requires particularly complex stage-management. Any alternative, such as

simple narration of the event could even be seen as a way of negating
its significance. This is illustrated with particular clarity in the
second chapter where Nkolo Mendo's narration of the news to
Meka's brother-in-law, Engamba, is depicted (*2*, pp.36–44).
Throughout this scene there is a concern for the ceremonial, almost
ritualistic aspects of narration. It is portrayed as a communal activity
governed by clear rules as we can judge from the way the scene
unfolds. The stranger waits for his audience to assemble and settle in
Engamba's *case* and then defers the moment of delivering his news
through a series of delaying tactics intended partially to increase
suspense but also perhaps to mark the gravity of what he is about to
say: he takes snuff, enquires after the presence of the village chief
and, after an exchange of vacuous proverbs, begins his narration with
an excessively detailed account of his personal reasons for the recent
trip he has made to Doum and from whence he brings news.

This is not so much a style of narration as an illustration of the
set of rules governing narrative practice and their connection to a
whole range of associated social practices. The news is seen as the
property of the whole village and its telling is a shared experience in
which other villagers, such as Mbogsi, have at least as great a part as
Engamba himself. Its telling is also linked to customs governing
hospitality: the teller is welcomed and made to feel at home before
being invited to speak. Afterwards he is offered food and accompanied on his way by his host. The practice of narrative is thus
associated with other practices and indeed with other narratives, as
though fundamental principles of Aristotelian poetics concerning
beginnings, middles and ends are far more problematic in an African
context.

It is certainly the case that the act of narration appears to
secrete other narratives. Nkolo's news leads him to recount his own
narrative of the whys and wherefores of his trip to Doum. On a
different narrative level, Nkolo's visit leads Engamba to reflect on
his own early years, on how his marriage to Amalia came about and
how he first met Meka. This interior monologue acts like an
accretion to the principal narrative and repeats the tendency to resort
to flashbacks and anticipatory reflections that I have already

identified as a feature of the narrative technique in the first chapter of the novel. If a further example were needed, I would refer readers to Amalia's reflections on her own childhood (2, pp.64–65) which are sparked off by the large number of baskets she expected to carry as she and Engamba set out for Doum. But there are numerous other examples of such brief intercalated narratives, particularly when Oyono portrays the Africans in a relaxed social setting.

The case of Nkolo Mendo nevertheless offers a clear illustration of the narrative technique favoured by Oyono in this novel. The event which is like the grain of sand in the oyster is the decision to award a medal to Meka. This event acts as an 'irritation' to the whole African community in the sense that it excites comments, reactions, discussions and narrations — so many accretions which, irrespective of their relevance to the original event, eventually produce the pearl that is the novel as a whole. It is only if we recognise the contribution of these other instances of narration that we can come to understand the extent to which *Le Vieux Nègre et la médaille* is a portrait of African *mores*, and although it may offer a critique of colonialism it is by no means a general critique but one which comes from a particularly African perspective. This point can perhaps be further illustrated by reference to another aspect of narrative technique, namely Oyono's clear preference in this novel for direct dialogue between characters over other forms of narration. The frequent recourse to scenes where dialogue is prominent conveys a particularly African flavour into the novel, as the rhythms and lexis of everyday speech can thus be faithfully reproduced. Clearly, this narrative technique was not really an option for Oyono in *Une vie de boy* since it sits ill with the decision to opt for a narration in the form of a personal diary. In his second novel, however, direct dialogue and other forms of direct verbal performance, such as Meka's speech at the *Foyer africain* and the subsequent speeches by the African chiefs, are important contributions to the development of the narrative. Indeed, the opening and closing chapters of the novel involve scenes in which Meka and his friends carry on discussions long into the night.

Perhaps by way of contrast to these narrative techniques which emphasise African qualities, the narrative structure of the novel has something decidedly classical about it. The division of the novel into three parts globally follows a strictly chronological organisation and focuses attention on the award ceremony held on 14th July as the central moment, while the first part describes the preparations leading up to this crisis point and the third part recounts the aftermath. As well as mapping a clear chronology, the three parts describe an essentially dramatic movement. The setting of the opening chapters alternates between Doum and Zourian, as Minyono-Nkodo points out (*21*, p.18), just as the principal characters in these chapters are alternately Meka and Engamba. Their eventual convergence, as Engamba and Amalia journey to Doum for the ceremony, increases the sense that the reader is witnessing a build-up of dramatic tension. The second part, recounting the detail of the ceremony itself and the reception at the *Foyer africain* which follows it, is the dramatic climax of the novel. In this section the narrative exposes the discrepancy between the Africans' naive faith in the colonialist rhetoric and the unchanging realities of colonial administration. The third part provides a resolution of these various tensions. There seems to be no evidence of anything having altered as far as the Whites are concerned but much has altered for the Blacks. Meka, once again in this respect the exemplary representative of his people, finally loses his illusions about the Whites and arrives at a lucid evaluation of his experience, not only with regard to the medal but more significantly with regard to the truth about his place in the colonial system. The sense that the various tensions have been resolved is underscored by the pervading harmony of the penultimate chapter when Meka symbolically returns to his African origins as he literally goes home to his *case*. But there is, of course, no resolution of the socio-political tensions amidst which he must continue to live and which are inherent in Oyono's portrayal of colonialism.

In both *Une vie de boy* and *Le Vieux Nègre et la médaille*, aspects of narrative technique and the ways in which Oyono chooses to structure his narrative contribute to the particular effects he is seeking to achieve in these novels. But as we have seen in relation to *Le Vieux Nègre et la médaille*, the emphasis on African narrative practice and on direct dialogue should serve to demonstrate that Oyono's purpose is never simply to attack colonialism. He is at least as concerned to project an image of Africa and Africans and to portray African realities. He does this possibly in a more marginal way in *Une vie de boy* than in *Le Vieux Nègre et la médaille* but the intention is unmistakably present in both novels. And nowhere is this duality of purpose more clearly in evidence than when we come to consider the range of comic effects Oyono employs and the targets at which he pokes fun.

## Comic effects

One of the most remarkable features of the two novels we are considering is the way Oyono manages to create comedy out of such fundamentally serious, and at times disturbing, subject matter. More recent works, such as *Le Pleurer-Rire* (1982) by the Congolese novelist, Henri Lopes, have continued to work this vein and treat in terms of tragi-comedy the disastrous humanitarian, political and social conditions in which so many Africans continue to live, long after the end of colonial rule. In the case of Oyono, the marriage of the comic and the tragic is by no means always successful. Indeed, in her study of African literature, Dorothy Blair is particularly critical of *Une vie de boy* in this respect and considers its humour as 'caustic' and 'lacerating'. She is much less critical of *Le Vieux Nègre et la médaille* which she judges to be an 'intensely comic novel' (7, p.227). The harsher judgement on *Une vie de boy* should probably be read as related to 'imperfections' I have already indicated in respect of narrative structure. Oyono certainly has difficulty in managing the change of tone from the narrator's early *insouciance* in the first *cahier* to the sadistic brutality which he must somehow inscribe into the second *cahier*. But whether or not Oyono successfully negotiates these difficulties is ultimately a matter of aesthetic judgement, and many readers would no doubt wish to contend that if the novel is aesthetically faulty — if *Une vie de boy* is 'not a completely satisfactory novel' as Blair puts it (7, p.225) — then this is the best way to illustrate the inevitable breakdown that must result from the tensions inherent in the forms of social organisation portrayed.

My purpose here is not to argue the satisfactoriness or otherwise of either of these novels, even in aesthetic terms, but to attempt to identify some of the methods by which Oyono sought to draw on comic effects as a way of increasing the impact of his work on the public(s) he was targeting. In this respect, Oyono can be placed firmly within a satirical tradition stretching back to the Juvenal of Classical antiquity and which, in a different age and circumstances, blossomed in the comedies of Molière. The comparison is not inappropriate, not least because Oyono's own involvement in the theatre (see *16*, pp.4–5) possibly explains his evident taste for the burlesque and for situations bordering on the farcical. In any event, there can be little doubt that Oyono exploits theatrical and comic effects very consciously in order to force his readers, whatever their allegiances, to recognise the ridiculousness of aspects of the behaviour and temperament he describes: the hypocrisy and moral posturing of the Whites, the gullibility and garrulousness of the Blacks and the incongruities which arise from their cohabitation.

The way Oyono exploits the notion of the incongruous is probably the most common source of comic effect in the two novels. In this respect, he repeatedly manages to turn to his advantage the fact that he is working on two registers: on the one hand, describing two different life styles and sets of expectations and, on the other, addressing his narrative to readers from two different cultural backgrounds. Thus, in many cases, the sense of incongruity is arrived at through exploiting to the full the differences in cultural behaviour which distinguish the Blacks from the Whites. A prime example in *Une vie de boy* is the scene in which Toundi discovers condoms under Madame's bed while sweeping the floor of her bedroom. To her fury, the naive Toundi indiscreetly examines the small rubber bags inquisitively and uncomprehendingly. There are strong elements of bawdiness and farce in this scene, as well as a good deal of plain irreverence which serves temporarily to unsettle the way power is distributed within the master-servant relationship. But when the scene is commented on by the other servants, the mockery focuses on cultural difference: in this instance, the Whites' obsession with clothing nakedness wherever it appears and their use of dress as a way of appearing distinguished:

> — Ces Blancs! S'exclama-t-il [le cuisinier], avec leur manie d'habiller tout, même leurs... [...].
> — Paraît que c'est pour faire bien... Ils mettent ça comme ils mettent leur casque ou les gants... (*1*, p.134)

Clearly, much of this humour is less effective today read against the background of an Africa severely affected by the spread of AIDS, but at the time of writing it could only be seen as scathingly disrespectful. Although there is much less of the knockabout comedy in it, much the same analysis would also apply to the scene in which Baklu complains of having to wash Madame's sanitary towels. Once again the aim seems to be simultaneously to scoff and undermine the myth of White superiority. This time, however, the commentary is more explicitly cultural and openly bemoans the fate of Blacks caught up in the snares of colonialism:

> Que diraient nos ancêtres s'ils voyaient que c'est nous qui lavons ces choses chez les Blancs!
> — Il y a deux mondes, dit Baklu, le nôtre est fait de respect, de mystère, de sorcellerie... Le leur laisse tout en plein jour, même ce qui n'a pas été prévu pour ça...
> (*1*, p.123)

Counterbalancing such scenes in which the Whites appear to be targeted are, for example, references to the Blacks' predilection for porcupine (*1*, p.20) or viper (*2*, p.33), which are not in themselves laughable but become comic when taken out of their cultural context or placed in sharp contrast with other cultural practices. A similar process of cultural decontextualisation operates in all the efforts Meka makes in his preparations for the award ceremony: the buying of the 'zazou' jacket and the attempt to force his feet into European-

style leather shoes. These are sources of comedy because of the way
they play on the incongruity of Meka's behaviour. The issue is not
that an African is seeking to adopt the costume and manners of the
Whites but that he is seeking to enter a world he does not understand
and on terms which are not his own. This is borne out by his
vulnerability in such situations, firstly at the hands of Ela (*2*,
pp.57–62) and then of Mme Pipiniakis (*2*, p.88), both of whom take
advantage of Meka.

However, it would certainly be misguided to categorise the
numerous examples of incongruity in terms of supposed targets, be
they individuals or whole groups. The fact of the matter is that the
co-presence of two cultures in a single space is fertile ground for a
whole variety of absurd encounters, accidents and misunderstandings. Meka is well-intentioned in his efforts but this does not
save hime from becoming ridiculous, because the situation in which
he finds himself inherently has elements of the absurd about it.
Similarly, when Binama, following a widespread fashion, names his
second son De Gaulle, there is no suggestion that he has ironic
intentions. This nevertheless allows Oyono to produce a portrait of
'De Gaulle' which cannot simply be read as an innocent description
of a little boy while totally excluding any thoughts about the French
President of the day:

> A ces mots, De Gaulle, un doigt dans le nez, avança vers
> Engamba. On ne pouvait savoir quel était exactement
> son teint. Toute la poussière ocre de la cour, mêlée aux
> cendres du foyer et à l'huile de palme qui avait
> dégouliné sur son petit ventre ballonné avaient formé un
> enduit polychrome rayé de traces de gouttes d'eau. Son
> nombril, ferme et volumineux comme un sein de jeune
> fille, s'inclinait vers son petit prépuce noirci par le fond
> de marmite qu'il avait tenu entre ses jambes. (*2*, p.67)

I have already referred to Oyono's taste for unflattering portraits in
the context of narrative technique, where I suggested that his harsh
portrayals of his compatriots served as a guarantee of the impartiality

of the narrative voice. It is also the case that Oyono achieves a considerable amount of comic effect through the high-lighting of striking physical details. In *Une vie de boy* it is the Whites who are generally singled out for such treatment, especially the women. Madame Salvain figures early on in the text: 'Madame Salvain portait une robe de soie rouge qui mettait en relief son gros derrière en as de cœur' (*1*, p.48), while many others are portrayed in equally unflattering terms at the reception held to celebrate the arrival of the Commandant's wife to Dangan:

> La femme du docteur parut aussi plate qu'une pâte violemment lancée contre un mur. Les grosses jambes de Mme Gosier d'Oiseau étaient empaquetées dans son pantalon comme du manioc dans une feuille de bananier. Les demoiselles Dubois se ressemblaient comme deux sacs jumeaux. (*1*, p.76)

In *Le Vieux Nègre et la médaille*, however, where the emphasis is very much on the individualisation of African characters, Oyono is no more flattering in his portrayal of Meka's fellow villagers:

> Les hommes mûrs du village étaient venus veiller chez lui. Il y avait Nua qui était comme lui sans âge. Il était sec comme une viande boucanée et avait la mâchoire continuellement en mouvement. [...] Nti, lui, était remarquable par son éléphantiasis commençant. [...]
> Mvondo était le neveu de Meka. [...] Personne ne s'étonnait qu'à trente ans il fût sans cheveux, ridé et rugueux comme un vieux lézard.
> Evina [...] avait perdu sa dernière dent au service des Blancs. Sa bouche s'était affaissée en rabattant le menton sur le cou, ce qui faisait ressortir son nez aux narines tellement ouvertes qu'on y voyait la morve blanchâtre qui y stagnait. (*2*, p.24)

Such passages do not fit easily into a partisan reading of the novel according to which all the ills of mankind originate from the White colonialists and are visited upon the Black victims. Instead they suggest a far more subtle and complex attitude on the part of the author towards his material and perhaps a desire to remain aloof from it as far as possible. There is something rather cruel about Oyono's insistence on the scandalously decrepit and dilapidated characteristics of Meka's friends. Certainly he does not seek to make them endearing either physically or morally, since they appear as weak in intellect and judgement as they are in body. There is a comic side to this catalogue of portraits but in such instances, when there is no clearly discernible satirical intent and the accumulation of details appears gratuitous, it is the comedy of the grotesque.

By way of contrast, the unprepossessing features of the 'Chef des Blancs' who carries out the awards ceremony are quite a different matter. As he kisses the cheeks of Pipiniakis, his own fat jowls wobble uncontrollably and he sweats profusely in the heat:

> Chaque mouvement faisait trembler le dessous de son menton semblable à un vieux sein couleur de latérite. [...] Selon qu'il ouvrait ou fermait les lèvres, sa mâchoire inférieure s'abaissait et se relevait, gonflant et dégonflant le dessous de son menton. [...] Le Chef des Blancs transpirait comme un lutteur. On eût dit que la pluie était tombée sur son dos. Une grande plaque humide s'étendait de ses épaules jusqu'à ses fesses. (*2*, pp.102–03)

No doubt such a powerful personage must be considered fair game for such treatment. Whether or not readers attempt to connect these unattractive physical attributes to moral categories (perhaps gluttony, indolence or undisciplined intemperance), the portrait remains profoundly disrespectful. As in earlier examples, when Oyono pokes fun it often serves to challenge the power relationships which normally obtain in the colonial setting. This particular instance is put to other purposes, however. At the ceremony Meka simply takes note of these features and only later does he see the resemblance between the 'Chef des Blancs' and the sow which habitually rummages around the makeshift latrine near his *case*:

> La truie se dandina en s'approchant de lui. [...] Meka demeura interdit. Où avait-il vu ce profil? Il hoqueta d'un rire qui l'arracha du sol. [...]
> — Je vois, haleta-t-il. [...] Ce profil est bien celui du Chef des Blancs... (*2*, p.160)

The comedy here is a vehicle for a more serious point: Meka's recognition of the piggishness of the 'Chef des Blancs' is symbolic of a more general recognition that the whole colonial system is motivated and perpetuated by various forms of greed.

One feature of this particular comic portrait and the associations it draws upon is its robust earthiness. Oyono is never slow to draw on scatological or sexual references as a way of achieving full comic effect, as many of the examples thus far have illustrated. It could be argued that Oyono's frequent crudeness is simply part of a realistic portrayal of an essentially rural society and of people who have remained closer to nature than their European counterparts. In *Une vie de boy*, the healthy interest in sex displayed openly by many of the Black characters (for example Sophie: *1*, pp. 67–68, and Kalisia: *1*, p.144) may have a comic directness about it, but it is also intended to contrast sharply with the more circumspect and more hypocritically prudish attitude of the Whites.

The robustness of Oyono's humour is also reflected in his tendency to exploit fully the potential for farcical development of many of the situations he describes. The scenes relating to Engamba's goat, Ebogo, in *Le Vieux Nègre et la médaille* are a case in point. The goat becomes so attached to its master that it remains in the *case* and even begins to feed on his bedding before Engamba finally decides to expel it (*2*, p.49). Such scenes, as well as scenes depicting Engamba hiding behind the door of his *case* in order to be able to enjoy his breakfast without having to share it with a troublesome neighbour (*2*, p.36), have something of the pantomime about them. This is partly owing to the fact that Oyono frequently refers to gestures and facial expression as a way of underlining the ludicrousness of a character or a situation. An example from *Une vie de boy* is the grimacing of the agricultural engineer as he simultaneously struggles with his jealousy and tries to wake up after a poor night's sleep:

> Il devint tout rouge. Cela contrastait avec son teint anémique de l'instant précédent. Ses yeux rivés sur les miens, il semblait avoir oublié le monde. Un tic fit trembler les commissures de sa bouche très fine. C'était une grimace inimitable qui eût déchaîné le rire d'une veuve à l'enterrement de son second mari. (*1*, p.71)

This latter example connects with yet another source of comic effect commonly exploited by Oyono: the misunderstandings and misconceptions that frequently mark the relationships across the colonial divide. In this scene, Sophie completely misreads the situation and mistakenly believes the engineer to be fooling around in order to amuse herself and Toundi. Elsewhere, the source of the misunderstanding is often attributable to the way a cultural difference impacts on linguistic usage. Kalisia misunderstands Madame's question when asked whether she has ever been a 'femme de chambre' and believes she is being asked if she has ever lived as a concubine with a man. Luckily Toundi is on hand to translate Madame's true meaning into the hybrid form 'boy de chambre' and the mistake is rectified (*1*, p.143). A further example of verbal confusion is provided when Mekongo recounts the occasion during the war when he slept with a White prostitute. During the encounter he misconstrues the term of endearment 'mon petit poulet' as an insult and comes close to assaulting the woman physically, before she convinces him of his mistake (*1*, p.92). These occasions, when Blacks misunderstand the language or behaviour of the Whites, are offset by a number of occasions when the Blacks purposely play on the lack of any mutual comprehension between the two groups in order to make fools of their masters. I have already mentioned the way Ondua, the tom-tom player, mocks the Whites in his song. In far less funny circumstances Mendim me Tit, the prison guard, also deceives the Whites when he merely pretends to beat Toundi and instead smears him in bull's blood while telling him to cry out in supposed pain (*1*, p.164). In similar vein, Meka is less than forthright in the way he conceals his penchant for alcohol from his confessor, or prepares to hide the fact he has been drinking by claiming he has been sucking an orange (*2*, p.15). Common to all these examples of mutual misunderstanding, accidental or willed, is the way they introduce an anarchic element into the impetus for order and control that typifies the colonialist attitude. In the latter examples especially, the readiness on the part of the Blacks to dupe their White masters is reminiscent of a fairly stock source of comic effect to be found in many literary genres and in many historical periods. Subjecting social inequities and injustices to ridicule, in the full gaze of the public eye, is probably as effective a tactic as any for the would-be righter of wrongs.

## Irony and satire

Such an impulse is, of course, satirical and, as we have already had occasion to recognise, the two novels under consideration provide ample material to illustrate this aspect of Oyono's writing as well as the various forms of irony upon which it inevitably draws. I have already had occasion to mention the fact that both Toundi and Meka are, initially at least, willing colonial subjects and the most basic irony of all derives from the scenario which both novels illustrate in their different ways: even such utterly compliant subjects are eventually destroyed or alienated by the representatives of the colonial system. But Oyono is no writer of political tracts and it is for this reason no doubt that his prime targets in both *Une vie de boy* and *Le Vieux Nègre et la médaille* are not the evils of colonialism as a system so much as the shortcomings of the petty-minded administrators and churchmen who serve that system and benefit from it, while pretending they are defending some high ideal of civilisation and working for the benefit of the colonised. The whole gamut of moral deficiencies the Whites exhibit, especially in *Une vie de boy*, serves to locate Oyono's criticism of colonialism firmly in an ethical and moral perspective rather than on social, political or economic grounds.

Certainly, the emphasis in *Une vie de boy* is on denouncing the White colonialists. Nevertheless, the fact that the Whites are the main target for satirical treatment should not mask from the reader the extent to which Oyono also consistently pokes fun at the Blacks. The following passage, in which Toundi provides an account of the funeral of Père Gilbert, is an interesting case in point:

> Il y avait là tous ceux qui voulaient montrer leur attachement au père défunt: hommes de peine aux larmes difficiles et dont les grimaces témoignaient des efforts qu'ils faisaient pour que l'émail de leurs yeux devînt humide, catéchistes au regard bête qui caressaient mollement leur chapelet, catéchumènes un peu mystiques qui escomptaient peut-être un miracle auquel ils auraient la chance d'assister, manœuvres dont l'air malheureux obligera sûrement le père Vandermayer à leur compter ce jour dans leur paye. Il y avait aussi tous ceux qui n'avaient jamais vu le cadavre d'un Blanc et encore moins celui d'un prêtre blanc; ils étaient les plus nombreux. (*1*, p.29)

As usual, Toundi sets the scene with a relatively uncomplicated and uncontroversial statement suggesting that those present have come to the funeral to express their fondness for the deceased. But when he goes on to provide further detail and to list the various categories of people attending, there emerges a sharp contrast between what Toundi originally assumed to be their motivation and the reasons for their presence which his own narrative implicitly or explicitly catalogues. It is worth noting in passing that this is yet another example in which Toundi's ostensible naivety is at odds with the more deeply cynical content of his narrative. In the event, none of the Blacks seems to express the simplicity of motive Toundi ascribes to them. Among the labourers grimacing in their struggle to shed a tear, the stultified catechists and the religious novices vaguely hoping they will witness a miracle, among the hired hands desperately trying to look miserable so as not to have their day's pay deducted by Père Vandermeyer and the remainder of the assembly who have come out of idle and misplaced curiosity, there is not a single participant who appears to confirm Toundi's original view.

A key element of even this short passage is once again Toundi's naivety. His opening statement to the effect that those attending the funeral were present because they wished to express their fondness for the priest suggests the existence of a harmonious set of relationships within the colonial setting: the implication is that the faithful Blacks are gratefully and respectfully paying tribute to a dedicated colonial worker. This stereotyped premise, which might well be the official view that the administration itself would be keen to propagate, could be considered as a typical example of the 'first meaning' which Toundi fairly consistently proposes for most of the events he witnesses. Once his own testimony begins to fill out the picture, this 'first meaning' is contested, thwarted and undermined either through an accumulation of contradictory details or through the very language Toundi employs (e.g. 'catéchistes au regard bête qui caressaient mollement leur chapelet') and the text effectively generates a series of other meanings which the reader cannot ignore even if Toundi seems oblivious to them. This pattern is repeated throughout *Une vie de boy*, and although in *Le Vieux Nègre et la médaille* the naivety is dissociated from the act of narration and incorporated into the substance of the narrative, the same process is at work. Hence, a good deal of the irony to be found in both novels can be traced back to the disparity that exists between the naive interpretation of events commonly proposed by Toundi and Meka and the more cynically realistic interpretations which the two novels simultaneously propose.

In *Le Vieux Nègre et la médaille* the satirical treatment that is meted out to the Blacks is far more fully developed than is ever the case in *Une vie de boy*, no doubt because in the second novel the emphasis switches from focusing essentially on White society to providing a far more detailed portrayal of the Blacks. In the event the satire may have a far more playful tone than in *Une vie de boy*, and at times even border on the farcical, as in the scenes involving Engamba and his goat, but the overall picture that emerges is a distinctly negative one. As Enama Eloundou comments in his 'Notes de lecture' on *Le Vieux Nègre et la médaille*:

> Cette image négative du colonisé est d'autant plus accentuée que les représentants de ce dernier dans le roman ne sont que de vieux paysans, des 'hommes mûrs' plus attentifs aux traditions ancestrales qu'aux réalités cachées du système dans lequel ils vivent. (*14*, p.121)

This targeting of the elderly, uneducated peasant classes naturally embraces Meka himself since he is, in every respect, the prime representative of the group. In many respects, the sheer foolishness of Meka and his fellow villagers is symbolically redeemed by the lucidity which Meka eventually acquires as a result of his experiences. It is, for example, the group as a whole which shares Essomba's final ironic joke about the Whites and their medal when he suggests that Meka should have presented himself before the 'Chef des Blancs' dressed only in his 'bila' (*2*, p.185–86). But it would be wrong to allow this comic finale to colour all that has preceded it, as though the satirical treatment to which Oyono has subjected the villagers were somehow rendered null and void by their own peals of laughter. The greater part of the novel pours scorn on the gullibility, the garrulousness and the ineffectuality of the Blacks and indicates quite clearly just how these weaknesses make them perfect fodder for the cynically manipulative forces of colonial rule. Nor, in my view, is Oyono particularly castigating a particular generation of his compatriots for a failure of political will. When Eloundou continues his 'Notes de lecture' with the comment: 'si le colonisateur doit réviser ses méthodes et sa mentalité, le colonisé devrait lui aussi se guérir de ses faiblesses et sortir de sa torpeur maladive' (*14*, p.121), he is no longer giving an account of Oyono's work, instead he is offering a private reaction to a reading of Oyono and suggesting a use that might be made of the novel. In short he is identifying possible solutions to problems which Oyono is quite content merely to describe. The difference is important. In his novels, Oyono is a satirist and not yet the politician he was later to become.

## Language and style

The present chapter began by raising a number of questions about the presumed readership Oyono may have had in mind when writing his novels. In actual fact, such questions are themselves largely rhetorical and serve merely to illustrate some of the complexities of the African literary scene and of postcolonial literatures in general. Similar questions could be asked about the 'choice' of language in which African authors write or the way such 'choices' relate or fail to relate to wider questions of linguistic competence and usage among potential readers. Reduced to its essentials the question might be phrased as follows: if the writer's purpose is to offer an African view of African experiences destined for an African audience then why 'choose' to write in French rather than an African language? The answer is, of course, that novelists like Oyono have little alternative but to eschew the use of their mother tongue and write in the languages of their former colonial masters, given the complexities of the linguistic landscape they inhabit. It is estimated, for example, that some two hundred and forty different languages are spoken in Cameroon (see *14*, p.6). Although the country has two official languages, French and English, pidgin English is widely used as the sole language of communication between large numbers of the population. Multilingualism is nevertheless a fact of life in Cameroon, as indeed it is throughout Africa, and a working knowledge of half a dozen languages is commonplace. Flexibility and a willingness to adapt to changing linguistic conditions are clearly evidenced in Oyono's own family since his father, who had been educated in German and had originally worked for the German colonial administration, saw himself obliged to re-enter the school system in order to acquire competence in French and so continue his career under the French colonial administration installed after the First World War (see *21*, pp. 3–4).

Such tenacity in the drive to acquire European languages reflects what would now be called their 'economic' importance, but it also reflects the practicalities of life and the fact that certain areas of activity, (particularly those involving writing, such as administration, schooling, judicial and legal matters), were the preserve of the French (or English) language. As a result, the numerous African languages of Cameroon have remained essentially vehicles of oral communication and although in the past they supported the wide range of cultural activities expressed through oral rather than literary means, there have been few attempts to transcribe many of these languages into written form let alone employ them in the production of literary texts, whether these be inspired by indigenous cultural practices or borrowed from the European tradition.[7] It would certainly be misguided to assume that Oyono had any real 'choice' when it came to writing his novels. In his own case the decision to write a novel at all is virtually synonymous with the 'decision' to write in French, given the particular time and place in which he lived. But it would be equally misguided to assume that any African novel written in French has a totally unproblematic relationship with the language it employs if only because, in the colonial (or postcolonial) context, the complex filiations that exist between any language and culture inevitably lack the directness and the immediacy that are usually taken for granted in more stable cultural conditions. It is perhaps for these reasons that within the canonical works of a given 'national' literary tradition, questions of style have so frequently been treated in terms of divergence from the norm. The concept of the stylistic norm, however linguistically defined or circumscribed, is merely a reflection of an even vaguer set of intuitions which together might be considered as constituting the cultural consensus. The transnational nature of, for example, African literature in French makes any such notion of cultural consensus

---

[7] For a brief survey of attempts at literary activity in the national languages of Cameroon see the article by David Ndachi-Tagne, 'Le labyrinthe des langues' in *14*, pp.6–10.

impossible and any view of style which is even tentatively predicated on theories of 'divergence from the norm' is equally unworkable.

The cultural conditions from within which novels are produced, and to which they relate, partially condition their reception by the reading public. Hence it could be argued that an 'African' novel and a 'French' novel, both written in high register standard French of the mid-1950s, do not necessarily 'speak' the same language or operate in the same way for their readers and that the first is inevitably a hybrid form since it speaks from the shadow of another culture. In a sense this is true, both in relation to the linguistic issues I have mentioned but also in relation to the interplay of African and European cultural traditions that are involved. There is no long-standing historical foundation for novel-writing or the production of literary texts in countries such as Cameroon where the functions of literary activity in the European sense were historically met by a diverse range of oral practices: story-telling, incantations, songs, riddles, proverbs and so on. Hence, the 'African' novel in question can be seen as not only 'borrowing' a language and seeking to adapt it to new conditions, but also as 'borrowing' a totally alien form of cultural activity and transplanting it into a different setting. On the other hand, it could equally well be argued that even when viewed from within the European tradition, the novel is an essentially hybrid form, constructing its meanings by presenting a multiplicity of voices and registers and ultimately susceptible of as many readings as it has readers.

Whatever the relative merits of these arguments it is clear that in *Une vie de boy* and *Le Vieux Nègre et la médaille* the co-presence of contrasting styles and registers of language is a key feature of both texts. These frequently underline the humorous intentions of the author but they also reflect the more serious preoccupations that Oyono is simultaneously addressing as he lays bare the different types of fracturing that occur within the colonial setting. In *Une vie de boy* such stylistic contrasts often occur within the narrative voice itself, as evidenced for example in the range of levels of register employed and the stylistic variation which is discernible when various entries in Toundi's diary are compared. A simple, unadorned style tends to dominate in the opening stages of the novel, where Oyono favours simple lexis and syntax in order to reflect Toundi's immaturity. Relatively early on in the novel, however, a more sophisticated formal, even literary style emerges. Here, for example, is a short passage from mid-way through the first *cahier*:

> La matinée était fraîche. L'herbe était humide. On entendait le crépitement des palmiers qui s'égouttaient sur la tôle de la Résidence. Dangan prolongeait son sommeil sous la brume immaculée de ses lendemains de grande pluie. (1, p.57)

In this instance, the short simple factual sentences which open the paragraph serve to establish a rhythm to the prose which gradually becomes ampler and more poetic as the sentences lengthen and metaphor replaces literal denotation. The vocabulary too becomes more refined in tone and suggest an impressionistic sensibility awakening to a morning of considerable splendour. Whether this style of expression is appropriate for the young character who is supposedly writing the entry is debatable, of course, but what should not be missed is the way the lyrical tone of the narration is placed in such stark contrast to the brutality of events which immediately follow. Half a page later, without giving Toundi any warning or allowing him any time for preparation, in much the same way as he might give an order to a dog, the Commandant brutally orders him into the back of the pick-up: 'Monte, toi! me dit-il. Nous partons en tournée. Il fit claquer la portière et mit la voiture en marche. Je n'eus que le temps de sauter sur les valises' (*1*, p.58).

The arrival of Madame at the Résidence provides a further occasion for Toundi to give full vent to his lyrical tendencies and romantic sensibility:

> Mon bonheur n'a pas de jour, mon bonheur n'a pas de nuit. Je n'en avais pas conscience, il s'est révélé à mon être. Je le chanterai dans ma flûte, je le chanterai au bord des marigots, mais aucune parole ne saura le traduire.

> J'ai serré la main de ma reine [...]. Désormais ma main est sacrée, elle ne connaîtra plus les basses régions de mon corps. Ma main appartient à ma reine aux cheveux couleur d'ébène, aux yeux d'antilope, à la peau rose comme de l'ivoire. Un frisson a parcouru mon corps au contact de sa petite main moite. Elle a tressailli comme une fleur dansant dans le vent [...]. Son sourire est rafraîchissant comme une source. Son regard est tiède comme un rayon de soleil couchant. (*1*, p.74)

The language of this extract has something of the parody about it, so outrageously effusive is Toundi's reaction to the handshake. The passage accumulates stereotypical imagery and references to idealised, not to say poeticised, nature in a completely unrestrained fashion. The overall effect is one of hyperbolic exaggeration which could easily be read as self-mocking in tone. Only the alibi of Toundi's youth and extreme naivety makes a non-ironic reading possible, but even if the passage is read without irony, as a sincere expression of emotion, it contrasts rather sharply with the more matter of fact narrative voice of the surrounding entries. In the wider context of events recounted in the novel as a whole, there is nevertheless, of course, a distinct irony about Toundi's admiration for Madame since she will eventually prove instrumental in his destruction. The variations in style identified here within the narrative voice itself would appear to be working at least partially to reinforce the significance of the events narrated.

Such contrasts and stylistic variations are also a feature of the content of the narration, however, since Toundi's role as observer and reporter leads him frequently to represent the actual speech as well as the reported speech of various characters. When the guard at the Résidence comments on the relative prowess of the Commandant and Gosier d'Oiseau in administering a boot up the backside, he does so in virtually incomprehensible 'petit nègre': 'Movié (1)! S'exclama le garde, Zeuil-de-Panthère cogner comme Gosier d'Oiseau! Lui donner moi coup de pied qui en a fait comme soufat'soud... Zeuil y en a pas rire...' (*1*, p.40). The explanatory footnote (1) to the effect that 'Movié' is a deformation of 'Mon vieux! (en petit nègre)' is presumably intended to help those unfamiliar with this register of language, although its presence in the text at all is no doubt intended for comic effect. The cook also uses very approximate French when vaunting his own culinary merits to Madame: 'Il baragouina qu'il avait trente ans de métier et que 'lui y en a touzou bon ksinier'' (*1*, pp.74–75), while the Commandant in a rather more sinister and certainly less playful tone openly mocks Toundi by adopting this style of speech during their first interview (*1*, p.34). The racist undertones in the Commandant's mockery are not understood by Toundi, who finds the scene incredibly funny. And the same combination of comedy and mockery with regard to poor linguistic competence is to be found in the scene which describes the schoolchildren's reception of the Commandant during his tour of duty in the bush:[8]

> Les élèves chantèrent d'une seule traite dans une langue
> qui n'était ni le français ni la leur. C'était un étrange
> baragouin que les villageois prenaient pour du français et
> les Français pour la langue indigène. Tous applaudirent.
> (*1*, p.63)

All of these examples focus on various uses of 'petit nègre' partially for comic effect but also as a way of shedding further light on aspects of the colonial relationship.

What these examples of the use of 'petit nègre' also highlight is the radical difference between the style(s) of language which typify the narrative voice and the styles of language which Oyono either reproduces or portrays in his efforts at characterisation. By and large the register and the stylistic features which are typical of the

---

[8] It should be mentioned in passing that the way this scene is recounted is yet another clear example of the supposedly inexperienced young narrator voicing opinions of a sophistication beyond his years. It thus provides a further illustration of the difficulty facing Oyono in his choice of an innocent young boy as his mouthpiece. At such moments as this, when Toundi speaks, the authorial voice is clearly discernible in the words he utters.

narrative voice in *Une vie de boy* are not vastly dissimilar to those which characterise the third person narration in *Le Vieux Nègre et la médaille*. In both cases Oyono employs standard French with relatively few instances of deviation from correct grammatical usage or syntax, unless he is purposely seeking to achieve stylistic effects such as those referred to above or is mimicking the speech patterns of particular characters. The past historic tense is frequently used in narrative sequences, underlining the rather staid and formal qualities of the narrative style. If anything, the modern reader may find the vocabulary and range of constructions associated with the narrative voice somewhat dated, despite Oyono's readiness to incorporate mildly obscene and scurrilous language when it is appropriate to the scenes he is describing.

No doubt this separation of styles is a feature of the hybridity I referred to above and reflects a dual ambition on the part of Oyono: on the one hand, his desire to work successfully within a recognised French literary tradition and to conform to the norms of that tradition and, on the other hand, to adapt the 'borrowed tools' of language and genre in such a way as to make them capable of expressing African realities for which they are not necessarily appropriate. Given the fact that *Le Vieux Nègre et la médaille* focuses far more on the African community than is the case in *Une vie de boy*, it is not surprising that examples of linguistic interference and interaction are more common in Oyono's second novel than they are in the first, if only because the African characters are more fully developed and play a more central role in the second novel. Although *Une vie de boy* contains a transliteration of an expression in one of the national languages: 'Ngovina ya ngal a ves zut bisalak a be metua' (*1*, p.149), which is the insulting name given to the Commandant by the locals, there is far less of a conscious effort in the earlier novel to portray the flavour of Africanised French.

In *Le Vieux Nègre et la médaille*, however, there is a proliferation of proverbs and dialectal expressions, literal translations into French of indigenous phrases and sayings and African interjections and speech patterns, all of which ensure that the text is unmistakably marked by its African subject matter. Minyono-

Nkono's study identifies some twenty or so proverbs in the novel and many of these not only include references to the flora and fauna of Southern Cameroon, they also closely approximate to linguistic models provided by national languages employed among the Beti ethnic group of that region (see *21*, p.31). The importance of proverbs within the African oral tradition is enormous. Insofar as they are deemed to express the distilled wisdom of generations of experience, they carry considerable weight in argument or discussion, but they also have a function as a simple adornment to discourse. Read within the context in which they appear in the novel, each of the following examples fulfils both of these roles: 'La marmite dans laquelle on a préparé le bouc garde longtemps son arôme' (*1*, p.103) 'Si tu veux savoir ce qu'un ami pense de toi, bois quelques gobelets avec lui' (*1*, p.119) 'Le chimpanzé n'est pas le frère du gorille' (*1*, p.168). Equally as numerous as the proverbs are the idiomatic expressions which frequently appear in direct translation in the speech or reported speech of various characters. Some of these are relatively obscure and indeed Oyono provides a footnote in order to explain that the expression 'briser les pattes de l'antilope' (*1*, p.45) is the equivalent of a honeymoon. Other expressions are readily comprehensible in their context, such as Nkolo's reference to 'cette nouvelle que je porte encore dans mon ventre' (*1*, p.40) or Engamba's reflection that the youthful Meka was easily recognisable as 'un homme qui avait d'autres hommes derrière lui' (*1*, p.46). And when a passer-by greets Meka with the following expression: 'Tu es là-dedans! Ça, c'est danser [...] Huuuuuuiiiiiiii! Yaaaaaaaa!' (*1*, p.171), he combines an idiomatic indigenous expression with a typical Beti interjection. Further examples could be found on virtually every page of the novel (see *18*, pp.80–83).

The overall effect of this repeated representation of Africanised French, even alongside the standard register of the narrative voice, is that the unprepared reader may feel slightly disorientated, but it is to be hoped enriched. Apart from the proverbs and dialectal expressions mentioned above, there is also a certain amount of interference on the level of syntax, lexis and construction, as Oyono frequently has recourse to African turns of phrase both in the dialogue among the African, as one might fully expect, but also on the occasions when the narrative recounts the inner thoughts of characters such as Meka, Engamba and Kelara. The interaction between the African and French cultural traditions that such linguistic interference celebrates, not only endows the prose with a strongly African flavour, it also, in a sense, offers a form of dramatisation of the hybridity which is at the heart of the social reality which Oyono is depicting, and usually satirising, in his novels.

# Conclusion

At the time Oyono was writing his novels, the Republic of Cameroon did not yet exist as in independent state, and the French colonial administration continued to exercise a wide range of powers over the indigenous population. I have already mentioned the fact that Oyono's father suffered directly as a result of his son's literary endeavours and that he lost his job as a consequence (*21*, p.4). Clearly then, the very fact of writing from within such a context, even, somewhat ironically, from the relative protection of France, was not without risk and could not fail to influence the sort of work Oyono produced. It possibly accounts for his very real concern to provide a balanced picture and yet it goes some way to explaining the bitterness and pessimism which underpins much of his writing, particularly in *Une vie de boy*. At one and the same time, it leaves readers with little alternative but to acknowledge the courage required to 'write back' from the periphery of the colonies to the metropolitan centre.

By way of conclusion, it is probably worthwhile reflecting on the sorts of meanings which it is possible to ascribe to the two particular examples of 'writing back' which these novels constitute. It should perhaps be said in passing that, over the last four decades or so, neither of them has attracted the level of critical attention that they in equal measure deserve, although the reading public has ensured that they have nevertheless remained in view and accessible. But the meanings that can be ascribed to them can probably best be exemplified by isolating, and perhaps caricaturing, two contrasting types of response which I would like to outline here. The first is not very far removed from the reality of the actual critical response which the novels have provoked and seeks to place both *Une vie de boy* and *Le Vieux Nègre et la médaille* within the fold of something closely akin to mainstream French literature. The canons of taste that apply and the types of judgement that the novels elicit all tend to assimilate the works to a tradition which belongs to the metropolis. Of course, this leaves Oyono himself in a rather odd position, since the corollary of such views is a tendency to consider the author as in some way a 'naturalised' or fully acculturated Frenchman, as someone who mimics the cultural and linguistic forms of the metropolis with the mastery of a metropolitan and therefore has, to all intents and purposes, acquired that status. It may of course be the case that the author is involved in such a quest for the respectability and prestige that accrues from recognition by the metropolis, but this particular way of categorising the novels allows them to be largely deproblematised. They can all the more easily be confined within a historical period and their significance limited to that of meritorious portraits of a society which has long since disappeared. They are more likely to be read as entertaining documents referring to a bygone age, and the criticisms they articulate are all the more palatable because they seem to require no remedy, relating as they do to a vanished past. Within this perspective, the fact that they were written by a black Cameroonian can be seen as a mere quirk of circumstance of no particular relevance.

In contrast to this view it is possible to see the novels as testaments to another, far more complex story which is only now coming into full visibility as the explosion of critical activity loosely centred on the notion of 'postcolonialism' suggests new avenues of enquiry, different perspectives and new methodological approaches to texts. This particular story is far from over, and elucidating it requires a constantly renewed critical appraisal of the complex web of relationships of which the colonial relationship described in these two novels is merely symptomatic and exemplary. Central to this approach, or set of approaches, has been a theoretical stance deriving from the work of the French philosopher, Michel Foucault, which posits as axiomatic the interconnectedness of discourse, power, 'knowledge' and forms of representation. Within this perspective, 'knowledge' is a product of discursive activity rather than a passive object which discourse in some way articulates, and discourse itself is one of the forms of activity through which power is exercised.[9] When Edward Said writes of the importance of the 'power to narrate, or to block other narratives from forming and emerging' (*27*, p.xiii) he suggests that this is constitutive of the relationship between culture and imperialism. It is difficult to imagine Oyono quibbling with such sentiments. And certainly, the power to tell one's own story, as one sees fit, to tell it from within one's own cultural perspective to an audience partially composed of readers who are on the same wavelength but who are also looking over their shoulders to see how the audaciousness of the enterprise is being received by those readers on the other side of the cultural, political, social and economic divide, all these are indeed elements of a story about the reception of the text which is as fascinating as the fiction which feeds it.

These two novels by Oyono are significant within this particular story because they are very early examples of such 'writing back', and yet the problems they present have contemporary relevance. Toundi's 'theft' of the colonisers' language in order to expose the vacuousness and hypocrisy of colonial attitudes and the way Meka's experience relativises the dominance of colonial values by foregrounding alternative African value systems are *scenarios* which continue to speak to readers today because they cannot be understood outside of the search for dialogue with the Other. Perhaps mainstream literary activity, both in respect of its

---

[9] In *Surveiller et Punir*, for example, Foucault argues that power relations actually generate 'knowledge'. He writes, 'En bref, ce n'est pas l'activité du sujet de connaissance qui produirait un savoir, utile ou rétif au pouvoir, mais le pouvoir-savoir, les processus et les luttes qui le traversent et dont il est constitué, qui déterminent les formes et les domaines possibles de la connaissance' (p.32). Later in the same book, Foucault goes even further and argues that power relationships are constitutive of reality itself: 'En fait le pouvoir produit; il produit du réel; il produit des domaines d'objets et des rituels de vérité. L'individu et la connaissance qu'on peut en prendre relèvent de cette production.' (p.196). Cf. Foucault, M., *Surveiller et Punir* (Paris: Gallimard, 1975). But the preoccupation with the relationships interconnecting power, knowledge, discourse and forms of representation, is a constant feature of Foucault's work and informs his whole output.

production and its reception, is inevitably rather more of a monologue by comparison.

# Select Bibliography

## WORKS BY OYONO

1. *Une vie de boy* (Paris: Julliard, 1956). Edition used: (Paris: Presses Pocket, 1970)
2. *Le Vieux Nègre et la médaille* (Paris: Julliard, 1956). Edition used: (Paris: UGE 'Collection 10/18', 1979)
3. *Chemin d'Europe* (Paris: Julliard, 1960). Edition used: (Paris: UGE 'Collection 10/18', 1973)

## GENERAL STUDIES OF AFRICAN LITERATURE

4. Ackad, J., Le Roman camerounais et la critique (Paris: Silex, 1985)
5. Anozie, S.O., Sociologie du roman africain (Paris: Aubier, 1970)
6. Bjornson, Richard, The African Quest for Freedom and Identity (Bloomington and Indianapolis: Indiana University Press, 1991)
7. Blair, Dorothy S., African Literature in French (Cambridge: Cambridge University Press, 1976)
8. Chevrier, Jacques, Littérature nègre (Paris: Armand Colin, 1990)
9. Chevrier, Jacques, Littératures d'Afrique noire de langue française (Paris: Nathan, 1999)
10. Kane, Mohamadou K., Roman africain et traditions (Dakar: Nouvelles Editions Africaines, 1982)
11. Moore, Gerald, Twelve African Writers (London: Hutchinson, 1980)
12. Palmer, Eustace, The Growth of the African Novel (London: Heinemann, 1979)
13. Notre Librairie, 99 (1989), 'Littérature Camerounaise 1. L'Eclosion de la parole'
14. Notre Librairie, 100 (1990), 'Littérature Camerounaise 2. Le Livre dans tous ses états'
15. Sartre, Jean-Paul, 'Orphée Noir', Situations III (Paris: Gallimard, 1949), 229–286

## CRITICAL STUDIES OF OYONO'S WORK

16. Battestini M. & S., and Mercier, R., *Ferdinand Oyono* (Paris: Nathan, 1977)
17. Chevrier, Jacques, *Une vie de boy de F. Oyono* (Paris: Hatier, 1977)
18. Delmas, Philippe, *Le Vieux Nègre et la médaille* (Paris: Nathan, 1986)
18a. Gikandi, Simon, *Reading the African Novel* (London: James Currey, 1987)
19. Kibera, Leonard, 'Colonial contact and Language in Ferdinand Oyono's *Houseboy*', *African Literature Today*, 13 (1983), 79–97
20. Mendo Ze, Gervais, *La Prose romanesque de Ferdinand Oyono* (Millau: Presses Maury, 1984) (Doctoral thesis: Université de Bordeaux III, 1982)
20a. Miller, Christopher, *Nationalists and Nomads* (Chicago:University of Chicago Press, 1998)
21. Minyono-Nkodo, Mathieu-François, *Comprendre 'Le Vieux Nègre et la médaille'* (Paris: Saint-Paul, 1978)
22. Moore, G., 'Ferdinand Oyono et la tragi-comédie coloniale', *Présence Africaine*, 46 (1963), 221–233
22a. Offord, M., Ibnlfassi, L., Hitchcott, N., Haigh, S., and Chapman R., *Francophone Literatures* (London: Routledge, 2001)

## GENERAL WORKS ON POSTCOLONIAL STUDIES

23. Ashcroft, B., Griffiths, G., and Tiffin, H., *The Empire Writes Back* (London: Routledge, 1989)
24. Bhabha, Homi K., *The Location of Culture* (London: Routledge, 1994)
25. Moore-Gilbert, Bart, *Postcolonial Theory* (London: Verso, 1997)
26. Moura, J-M., *Littératures francophones et théorie postcoloniale* (Paris: PUF, 1999)
27. Said, Edward, *Culture and Imperialism* (London: Vintage, 1994)